The Song of Roland

DOVER · THRIFT · EDITIONS

The Song of Roland

ANONYMOUS

DOVER PUBLICATIONS, INC.
Mineola, New York

DOVER THRIFT EDITIONS

GENERAL EDITOR: PAUL NEGRI

EDITOR OF THIS VOLUME: TOM CRAWFORD

Bibliographical Note

This Dover edition, first published in 2002, is an unabridged republication of the 1919 second edition of the version published by Yale University Press, New Haven, in 1914. A new Note has been specially prepared for this edition.

Library of Congress Cataloging-in-Publication Data

Chanson de Roland
     The song of Roland / Anonymous; [translated into English verse by Leonard Bacon].
          p. cm.
     · Unabridged republication of the 2nd ed. published by Yale University Press, New Haven, 1919. With new publisher's note.
     ISBN 0-486-42240-2 (pbk.)
     1. Roland (Legendary character)—Romances. 2. Epic poetry, French—Translations into English. 3. Knights and knighthood—Poetry. I. Bacon, Leonard, 1887–1954. II. Title.

PQ1521.E5 B2 2002
841'.1—dc21

                                                                    2002017523

Manufactured in the United States of America
Dover Publications, Inc., 31 East 2nd Street, Mineola, N.Y. 11501

Publisher's Note

THE FIRST and greatest of French epic poems, *The Song of Roland* was composed about 1100 A.D. by an unknown poet, probably in northern France. It is one of the best of a medieval genre called *chansons de geste* (lit. "songs of deeds"), that told of heroes and battles and mighty feats of arms. The songs were usually recited aloud to the accompaniment of music for the entertainment of the nobility.

The Song of Roland is based on an actual historic event that occurred in the eighth century; however, by the time it was written down, the kernel of truth at its core had succumbed to generations of legendary accretion. The historic facts of the matter are these: Charlemagne (Charles the Great) invaded Spain in the year 778, hoping to take advantage of opportunities offered by dissension then rife among the Saracens who controlled the country. When those opportunities failed to materialize, Charles marched back the way he had come, through a pass in the Pyrenees Mountains. It was then that his rear-guard was attacked and annihilated at Roncevaux by Basques who lived in the mountains. Although they fought valiantly, every last man was killed, including Hrodland, Count of the Marches of Brittany.

Over the years, a body of legend grew up around this incident, which transformed the historic event into an occurrence of mythic proportions. Charlemagne, who was actually thirty-six at the time of the battle, in the chanson is an old man with flowing white hair; the Basques have become Saracens; the story turns on an invented plot of treachery by one Ganelon, brother-in-law of Charlemagne; and Hrodland is now Roland, a nephew of Charlemagne, with a faithful friend called Olivier and even a betrothed, Alda.

Although the exact date of its composition is unknown, the poem is believed to have been written around the time of the First Crusade (in 1095 Pope Urban II had appealed for help in taking back the Holy Land from the Turks and Arabs). Thus, *The Song of Roland* has been seen by some as a propaganda piece, designed to arouse the Christian West to battle against the Muslim "infidels." Whatever the reason behind its composition, its patriotic ardor, masterly versification and brilliant portrayal of gallant men and noble deeds have made it one of the great national poems and a landmark of Western literature.

The work consists of about 4,000 lines, in 298 laisses, or stanzas, of varying length, from three or four lines to a few hundred. The ten-syllable lines are linked by assonance (i.e. the last word contains a similar vowel sound but not necessarily a perfect rhyme), or by rhyme. The result is a tour de force of medieval poetry, notable for its freshness, directness and simplicity. What it may lack in subtlety and imaginative power the poem more than makes up for in an epic grandeur that captures the magnificence of clashing armies and the revelation of heroic spirits.

The Song of Roland is presented here in a free-flowing translation by Leonard Bacon that is eminently accessible to the modern reader, while retaining the spirit, flavor, and majesty of the Old French original.

Preface

AN APOLOGY for a new translation of the Song of Roland is perhaps not unnecessary. Several excellent versions in prose and verse already exist. It was with no view to supplanting them that the present volume was undertaken. But the writer feels certain that a work like the Song of Roland is susceptible of many interpretations. Hence he has not hesitated to attempt one of his own.

It is proper to indicate certain interpolations and certain deviations from the Oxford text on which the present version is based.

Laisses CXIIa, CXIIb, CXIVa, CXIVb, CXIVc, CXXVa, CXXVIIIa, CXXVIIIb, CXXVIIIc, CXXVIIId, CXLIVa, CLIVa, are supplied from other sources than the basic text, with a view to filling up certain lacunæ in the narrative.

Other interpolations and deviations are indicated in the notes.

It would be impossible to enumerate the various kindnesses shown me by others in carrying out this little adventure. I take great pleasure in acknowledging my indebtedness to Professor George Rapall Noyes who suggested this undertaking, to Professor Walter Morris Hart who made many crooked paths straight, and to Professor Rudolph Schevill who encouraged me in difficulty. Finally there is owing to my father, my mother, and my wife a debt of gratitude not to be expressed easily or in a preface.

Berkeley, California, 1914.

Preface to the Second Edition

THAT THIS little work has attained the distinction of a second edition must naturally gratify the translator. He has endeavored to reform such verses as appeared to him to halt, and has added a note on the date of the poem.

The last four years have endued with a greater dignity the noble poem that first revealed the meaning of France.

Berkeley, California, 1919.

Introduction

In an illuminating passage Gaston Paris has paid, once for all, his perfect tribute to the Song of Roland. "At the entrance of the Sacred Way," runs his exquisite statement, "where are arrayed the monuments of eight centuries of our literature, the Song of Roland stands like an arch massively built and gigantic; it is narrow, perhaps, but great in conception, and we cannot pass beneath it without admiration, without respect, or without pride." To one in any way acquainted with the poem further comment is unnecessary, but the uninitiated may feel that an elucidation of the beautiful and imaginative figure is desirable. What is this poem eight centuries old, written in incomprehensible French, about a forgotten episode, that it should thus stir the enthusiasm of a Professor of Mediæval Literature?

The finest and earliest of the Romance Epics deals with the treason of Ganelon, the brother-in-law of Charlemagne, who, sent on an embassy by the Emperor to Marsile the King of Spain, betrayed his nephew Roland, and the army under his command, to the Saracen. It relates the details of the battle of Roncevaux in which Roland, his comrade Olivier and their companions fell gloriously, the vengeance which Charlemagne exacted upon the false Spanish King and his overlord the Emir of Babylon, and concludes with an account of the trial by combat which resulted in the conviction and terrible execution of the traitor Ganelon. These are events of the poem; the details one will say of a spirited story, hardly more.

But there is far more than that to say. Few men living are qualified to trace the lineaments of racial and national feeling as they appear in this epic. But a sketch of the events which gave rise to the elaborate legend incorporated in the poem may help us to a kind of comprehension. On the 15th of August, 778, the rear-guard of the army which Charlemagne had led into Spain on an expedition, barren of any important result, was cut to pieces by the Basques in the Pass of Roncevaux in the Pyrenees. In this disaster Hrodland, Count of the March of Brittany, was slain. So small a spark of fact was to kindle three centuries later a great flame of splendid poetry.

Presumably the tiny ember was well nursed. It is more than probable that a popular balladry celebrated the courage of the brave soldiers who fell in the only great reverse suffered by the arms of Charlemagne. Evidence is cited by all authorities to prove the existence of a strong sentiment felt by the vulgar on the subject within sixty years of the battle. This being the case, what more natural than a spontaneous burst of military poetry dedicated to the martyr-soldier, and enhancing his exploits with every fresh emanation? Such a folksong it was doubtless that Taillefer sang at Senlac when he rode out ahead of the attacking army tossing his sword in air and catching it again.

But it was for a greater than Taillefer that the task of raising the subject to its proper dimensions was reserved. Who he* was we do not know. The internal evidence of the poem as to his special characteristics is of the most tenuous sort, yet a few details do appear. Probably he flourished in the latter half of the tenth or in the eleventh century. At any rate what appears to be a reference to Samuel the King of Bulgaria, who died in 1014 after a forty-year struggle with the Emperor Basil II, would seem to set a limit before which the poem could not have been written. The linguistic authorities favor the eleventh century. Again he was probably a layman. The hearty contempt which, in spite of a severe tone of piety, he expresses for monks in general, tends to prove the point. Again he was a man of remarkable learning. His geographical erudition was for the time extraordinary. He understood thoroughly the parliamentary and legal procedure of the period, the customs of the

---

*It is of course impossible to determine whether or not the Therould mentioned in the last line of the Song of Roland was the author of the poem. As the old story goes, it may have been written by another man of the same name. It is probable that the matter of the poem is derived from two or more sources. The episode of Baligant is obviously not *en train* with the rest of the story. However, there is the strongest reason for thinking that no matter where he obtained his materials the poem as we have it is the work of one man.

The attempts to discover various hands in a work concerning whose composition no external evidence exists seems to me on a par with the mad hypothesis of those who, not content with fathering all the plays of Shakespeare upon Francis Bacon, believe that he is also to be credited with works as dissimilar as the Jew of Malta and the Faerie Queen.

assemblies of free nobles, the manner in which "justice was done by
Charles the King." He was, furthermore, the ablest and most splendid
expositor of what is *par excellence* the most important idea of the
mediæval mind, the idea which was to the eleventh and twelfth cen-
turies what the theory of evolution is to ours.

The idea of feudalism as it was must not be confused with the idea
of feudalism as the novelists have conceived it. It was not a social the-
ory commingled of politeness and barbarity. Feudalism meant to the
era of William of Normandy an orderly system, far-reaching and all-
embracing. It meant a system relating man to master and master to
God. It placed responsibility, it made plain duty, it did justice. Perhaps
its methods were crude and its outlook narrow; but our social iniquities,
are they more courageously faced today? Our statesmen, are they more
far-sighted? The spirit of this feudalism raised to its highest power, con-
ceived in its noblest phase, is the informing spirit of the great poem
which we are considering. The performance to the uttermost of a
feudal duty is the highest deed a good man can do. Everything is to be
sacrificed to this end. It is on this subject that the poet is most magnif-
icently eloquent. And it is as an expression of this misunderstood but
glorious ideal that the poem is particularly interesting.

When the importance of this idea is fully realized it will perhaps
appear more clearly that the Song of Roland is something more than a
striking story. Consecrating the pursuit of the feudal ideal as it did, it
must have become an ethical force of a positive type. Who can say what
France may not have owed in her stormy formative years to a poem
which so triumphantly celebrated that loyalty and sense of national
unity of which the country stood in such bitter need? Is it too fanciful
to imagine that the Song of Roland received, nursed, and disseminated
the spirit whose purest exponent was to be Joan of Arc? At all events
France owes to her first and greatest epic the earliest example of that
patriotism, that fine tendency to act as an undivided nation, which has
made her a spiritual leader of the races of men.

Of the poetic qualities of the Song of Roland, the reader must form
his own opinion. M. Legouis in his delightful Défense de la Poésie
Française has described them and our English debt to them as only a
brilliant Frenchman can. The pleasure in color and light and sound,
the fine effects of contrast, the human touches which relieve a charac-
terization tending too much to resemble the rough-hewn sculpture of
the period, all these are earnest of greatness. The freshness and direct-
ness of the poet, his enthusiasm and simplicity are infinitely attractive.
On the other hand, the reader may find the repetitiousness and metic-
ulous attention to inconsiderable detail boring to a degree. He will
realize with a pang that the choosing of the twelve Saracen champions

involves a monotonous series of conflicts with the twelve peers. Nor will he be indemnified for his long-suffering by the perpetual harping repetition on the subject of Ganelon's treachery.

Nevertheless, the reader with patience to endure what was inexpressibly delightful to the eleventh century, will be repaid for his complaisance with magnificent pictures of flashing armies, with the epic revelation of heroic spirits, and finally with the sense of having been in the presence of what was intrinsically majestic, powerful and original.

THE SONG OF ROLAND

FOR SEVEN years together, the Emperor Charlemagne,
Our Lord and King, had sojourned within the land of
Spain.
From the upland to the sea-coast he had conquered all the
land
Nor was there any castle before him left to stand.
There was not town nor bulwark unbroken by his might,
Save only Saragossa that standeth on the height.
King Marsile held that city, in whom no grace was found
To love his God. He worshipped Apollo and Mahound,
Nor could shun the evil fortune that beleaguered him
around.

II. King Marsile of Saragossa to the orchard got him gone.
He laid him down in the shadow on a white marble stone.
About the King were gathered more than twenty thousand
men.
His counts and dukes unto him King Marsile summoned
then:
    "Hearken, my lords, how sorely are we girt with sin and
woe.
Here now is come King Charlemagne our land to overthrow.
I have no host of battle to meet him in his might,
Nor store enough of henchmen to beat him in the fight.
As wise men give me counsel. Save me from this death and
shame."
    None spake save Blanchandrin alone from Val Fonde
Keep that came.

III. Among the wisest heathen Blanchandrin was known to be.
And a good vassal, moreover, and a man of chivalry.
Cunning he was, and skillful his overlord to aid,
And he spoke unto King Marsile:
"Do thou not be dismayed.
But send unto King Charlemagne, the arrogant and strong,
Promise of faithful service and friendship leal and long.
Gifts shalt thou send unto him, both dogs and lions good,
And seven hundred camels, and a thousand hawks well mewed.
With the gold and with the silver, mules four hundred shalt thou load,
And fifty wains, moreover, to travel on the road,
Wherewith to pay his soldiers. He hath warred here long enow.
And unto Aix it behoves him in the land of France to go.
At Michaelmas thou shalt turn thee to Christ and his belief
To hold in truth and honor of the Emperor thy fief.
If for hostages he asketh, thou shalt for him procure
Of our children ten or twenty to make thy faith more sure,
And though thereby he perish, I will send mine own dear son.
Rather let them die straightway than that we should be undone
In honor and dignity, and go like beggars in the land."

IV. Said Blanchandrin, moreover:
"Now by this good right hand,
And by the beard that on my breast is beaten by the breeze,
Soon shall you see the French depart out of our provinces.
They will go back to the land of France and the country that is theirs.
And when each man among them to his own house repairs,
In Aix, in his own chapel, will sit King Charlemagne.
To Saint Michael will he proffer high festival again.
The day will come; the term will pass; no tidings will there be;
And the King's wrath is terrible, and a proud man is he.
And forthwith from our hostages the heads he will let smite.
Let them die, so Spain we lose not, the beautiful and bright,
Or ever bitter evil be forced to undergo."
Said the heathen: "Indeed the matter, it well might happen so."

V. Marsile the King had finished his council for the day.
And he summoned Claris de Balaguer and the men of his
array.
Estramaris and Eudropis his father there appeared.
And Priamos, moreover, and Guarlan of the beard,
And Machiner and Maheu (Machiner's eme was he),
.And Joïmer, and Malbien, the man from oversea,
And Blanchandrin, moreover, that counsel they might take.
Ten men of the most villainous he summoned, and he spake;
    "Lord barons, unto Charlemagne the King ye shall go
down.
He lieth in the leaguer of Cordova the town.
The branches of the olive in the hand ye all shall bear
That your good will and submission to the Emperor shall
declare.
And if through your good counsel ye may achieve a peace,
I will give you fiefs and ample lands, as much as you shall
please,
And enough of gold and silver."
                                    Then said the heathen men:
    "Enough we have already." He closed the council then.

VI. But he said unto his henchmen:
                                "My barons, ye must fare.
And in your hands the branches of the olive ye must bear.
Ye shall conjure the Emperor, when ye speak to him for me,
That on me he have mercy for his God's clemency.
The month shall not pass over, ere unto him again
I shall follow my embassadors with a thousand faithful men,
And be baptized his man to be in friendship and in truth.
And if he will have hostages, he shall have them in all sooth."
    Said Blanchandrin: "Fair fall thee for the tidings we
shall bring."

VII. Ten white mules were led out to them by Marsilies the
King,
The gift of the King of Seville. Their bits were all of gold.
The saddles set upon them were silver to behold.
They got them straight on horseback at Marsile his com-
mand—
The branches of the olive they carried in the hand.
And they came to Charles who governed the land of France
the fair,
Who could not wholly keep himself from falling in the snare.

VIII. The Emperor was merry; his heart was glad withal.
The town of Cordova was ta'en and overthrown the wall.
With his catapults the towers he had strongly beaten down.
His chevaliers much treasure had taken in the town.
Much gold and silver trappings exceeding rich and rare,
And longer in the city no men at all there were
That were not slain or Christian. In an orchard Charlemagne
Lay with Olivier and Roland and the nobles of his train,
Samson the Duke and Anseïs the fiery-hearted one,
And Geoffrey of Anjou, bearer of the King's gonfalon,
And Gerier and Gerin, and many a knight as good.
Full fifteen thousand Frenchmen were gathered in the wood.
The cavaliers were seated upon the cushions white.
They were playing at the tables for pastime and delight.
The wiser and the elder at the game of draughts they played;
But the light lads of the army great sport with fence they
made.
Under a pine beside a briar was lightly to behold
A high-seat nobly fashioned out of the purest gold.
There sat the King who governed all the sweet realm of
France,
White-bearded and with flowery hair; proud was his
countenance
And fair likewise, and his body was stout and big of bone.
To who would look upon him the King was lightly known.
And forthwith the embassadors descended from the steed,
And saluted him in friendship, and bade him well to speed.

IX. Blanchandrin spoke first to the King. He said:
                    "Now God thee save,
The glorious whom we must adore. King Marsilies the
brave
Putteth this matter to thee. He hath questioned long and
well
Concerning the religion that shall save him out of Hell.
He would give thee bears and lions, and in leash the grey-
hounds good,
And seven hundred camels, and a thousand hawks well
mewed.
And with the gold and silver, mules four hundred will he load,
And fifty wains, moreover, to travel on the road.
There will be bezants a-plenty of the fair gold and fine,
Wherewith thou mayst pay lightly the soldiers of thy line.

Here hast thou tarried overlong. It behoves thee to repair
To France, and Marsile's pledges shall soon pursue thee there
Thy faith will he take on him, and with hands folded amain
Become thy man, and hold of thee in fief the realm of Spain."
    Unto his God the Emperor lifted both hands of grace.
Forthwith he lowered his proud head, and the thoughts came
apace.

X. The Emperor bent down his brows. No hasty word he
spake.
In speech it was his custom his leisure aye to take.
But lordly was his visage when he lifted up the head;
And he spake to the embassadors:
                                    "Now much good have ye said.
But King Marsile for the chiefest of my foeman is renowned.
Upon his words that ye have given, what credit may I found?
Said the Saracen:
                            "Our hostages shall make thy trust the
more.
Thou shalt have ten or fifteen men, or, an thou wilt, a score.
And at the hazard of his life I will send mine own dear son.
The children of our bravest to thee shall be sent on.

And in thy lordly palace, what time that thou shalt be
On the great feast of Saint Michael-of-the-Peril-of-the-Sea,
There will my pledges follow (this is the word of the King)
At the baths that God wrought for thee will he have his
christening."
Then answered Charles the Emperor:
                                    "Yet hope abideth here."

XI. Oh, lovely was the vespertide, and the sun sank fair and
clear.
The ten white mules to the stables by Charlemagne were
sent.
Within the noble orchard the King let pitch a tent,
And host to the embassadors was Charlemagne that day.
Twelve sergeants of the army, their servitors were they.
They bided all the evening till the fair day was born.
The Emperor already was risen in the morn,
And had heard mass and matins. 'Neath a pine-tree did he
fare.

He called to him his barons to take his counsel there.
For he desired unto the Franks the matter to declare.

XII. Beneath a mighty pine-tree the Emperor sate in state.
He summoned there his barons to counsel and debate.
There came Archbishop Turpin; there, also, Ogier came;
Old Richard and his nephew that Henry had to name;
And Accelin the noble count of the land of Gascony;
Tybalt of Rheims, and Milon (of Tybalt's kin was he)
And Gerier and Gerin. With them Count Roland stood,
And Olivier, moreover, the gallant and the good.
Of Franks of France unto the place a thousand men did wend.
Ganelon came, the traitor that betrayed his King and friend.
And there began the council that had so ill an end.

XIII. "Lord barons," said King Charlemagne, "King
Marsile doth engage
To give me store of treasure out of his heritage,
Lions and bears, and greyhounds, well leashed that be and
good,
And seven hundred camels, and a thousand hawks well
mewed;
Four hundred mules that bear the gold of the Arabian plains,
And therebeside, moreover, full fifty laden wains.
But he layeth condition on me, that to France I shall repair.
Unto Aix will he follow, and in my palace there
By the law of our salvation clean christened will he be,
And hold in fief his marches and his domains of me.
But I know not what he thinketh, if it be good or guile."
   Thereto said the French barons: "We had best ward the
while."

XIV. The King made clear his counsel unto the barons there,
But Count Roland in the matter would have nor lot nor
share.
Up he sprang and gainsaid it:
                              "Never believe again
King Marsile. Seven years are past since first we came to
Spain.
Constantinople city, and Commibles the town beside,
Valtierra and the Land of Pine have I conquered far and wide.
Balaguer, Seville, Tudela, I stormed them in my way.
King Marsile will do nothing, but deceive thee and betray.

He sent thee fifteen Paynims; they also said the same.
With branches of the olive to speak their word they came.
Thou badest the Franks to council. They charged thee
light enow.
Two counts of thine to the heathen, thou badest then to go.
One of them was Count Basan, the other Basil the Count.
The heathen clave their necks for them 'neath Haltilie the
mount.
Carry out the war, King Charlemagne, in the guise that it
began.
Lead on to Saragossa the army of the ban.
Though the siege endure thy life-time, undertake it, Charle-
magne,
And avenge thy two embassadors that by this knave were
slain."

XV. The Emperor bowed down his head when spoke the
paladin.
Aye plucked he with his fingers at the beard on lip and chin.
He spake nor good nor evil to his nephew in reply.
The Franks were still. Ganelon rose, and to the King did cry.
But fierily and fiercely Ganelon his speech began.
He said unto King Charlemagne:
                                    "Believe no lawless man,
Nor me nor any other, if no gain to thee it bring.
But, when such a thing is promised by Marsilies the King,
That with hands joined together thy henchman he will stand,
And will receive the whole of Spain for a good gift at thy
hand,
And in the pathway of our faith will undertake to go,
Let us reject his counsel, that hath given counsel so.
For Sire, he careth little by what death we shall die.
And the counsel of this arrogance—for to us stand thereby
Would in no way be wisdom, nor just in any guise.
Let us forsake the foolish and cleave unto the wise."

XVI. Neimes came next. At the King's court was better
vassel none.
He said:
          "Ye have heard the answer of the Count Ganelon.
And wisdom hath he spoken, but this let all men know:
Marsile the King is beaten in the broad overthrow.
By storm, O King, hast thou taken his cities one and all;

With thy catapults, moreover, thou hast battered down his
wall;
Thou hast beaten his men in battle, thou hast burned his
cities with fire.
When peace and pity at thy hands King Marsile doth desire,
Sin would it be most certainly that battle should endure,
If he will give thee hostages to make his warrant sure.
Never must this great war of ours into a greater swell."
    Then said the Frankish barons: "The Duke saith right and
well."

XVII. "Lord barons," said King Charlemagne, "which one
of you shall bring
My message to Saragossa to Marsilies the King?"
    Neimes the Duke gave answer:
                        "I will go at thy command.
The staff of state and the gauntlet give now unto my hand."
    King Charlemagne said straightway:
                        "Too wise is thy heart within,
And by the beard upon my lip and the beard upon my
chin
Thou shalt not in this hour go so far away from me.
Go sit thee down, I prithee, since no man summons thee."

XVIII. "Lord barons," said King Charlemagne, "say now
which of my men
We shall send to Saragossa unto the Saracen
That ruleth in the city."
                      Roland his answer gave,
"I will go myself." Said Olivier:
                    "Too terrible and brave
Is thy spirit. And I fear me thou wouldst have some over-
throw.
but if the King desire it right gladly will I go."
                Said the King:
                "Peace! Nor he nor thou shall issue
from my sight.
For by this beard of mine ye see that turneth now to white
A judgment on my twelve good peers most certainly would
fall."
    Hushed were the Franks and silent they waited one and all.

XIX. Turpin of Rheims rose straightway from his station in
the ranks,
And said unto the Emperor:

                                    "Let be—let be thy Franks.
They have been here this seven year and suffered pain and
woe.
Give now the glove and staff to me. To the Paynim I will
go,
The realm of Spain that ruleth, his purposes to see."
    But the Emperor gave answer exceedingly angrily:
    "Sit down on the white cushion and speak no more this
day,
Unless I shall command thee thy counsel here to say."

XX. "Ye knights of France," said Charlemagne, "a baron of
my land
Choose ye now with my message in Marsile's court to stand."
    Said Roland:
                 "Let it be Ganelon that is near kin to me,
My stepfather." Then said the Franks:
                            "He might do it readily.
An thou send him, thou canst never send a wiser man than
he."

XXI. Said Charlemagne:
                 "Count Ganelon, now forth before us stand.
The staff of place and the gauntlet, now take them in the
hand.
Thou art chosen. By the common choice on thee the lot
doth fall."
    Said Ganelon:
                 "This matter Count Roland wrought it all.
In no wise do I love him, nor Olivier beside,
(For he is Roland's comrade) nor the twelve peers of thy
pride
That love Count Roland. In thy sight do I defy them now."
    Said the King:
                 "Too much of evil within thy heart hast thou.
But thou must go most certainly because of my command."
    "I go! but lo, I have thereto no warrant to my hand.
Basil and Basan the brothers no warranty had they.

XXII. "And I know that to Saragossa I needs must take my
way.
And he who goeth thither returneth never here.
Ah King, am I not wedded unto thy sister dear,
By whom I have a man-child, and fairer is none than he.
If the lad Baldwin liveth, a hero will he be.
To him I leave my honors and all my fiefs likewise.
Look to the lad, for never shall I see him with these eyes."
   Said Charlemagne the Emperor:
                                     "Too tender is thy heart.
But since I have commanded, it behoves thee to depart."

XXIII. And thereupon was Ganelon troubled exceeding
sore.
From his neck he snatched the mantle of marten-fur he wore.
And stood there in his silk attire. His eyes went to and fro
Proudly. Most splendid was his port, and his flanks were
stark enow.
And all the peers looked on him, so fair he was to see.
And he said to Roland:
                        "Wherefore, fool, is this folly come on thee?
For that I am thy step-sire lightly may all men know.
Yet hast thou given counsel that to Marsile I should go.
If but God grant it to me that I come back again,
I shall attempt against thee what shall bring thee grief and
pain
And shall endure moreover, unto thy life's last tide."
And the Count Roland answered:
                          "I have heard folly and pride.
Men know that for this menace I do not care a whit;
But the bearer of this message should be a man of wit.
In thy place, at the King's pleasure, I will go to compass it."

XXIV. But Ganelon gave answer:
                              "Thou shalt not go for me,
For I am not thy henchman; nor am I lord of thee.
The Emperor in his service has given me command.
I will go to Saragossa before the King to stand.
Leisure I need, for mine anger is risen high and proud."
   And when Count Roland heard it, he began to laugh aloud.

XXV. When Ganelon saw Roland how loud he laughed and
long,

It irked him. He was like to burst, his anger was so strong.
He had lost his wit in a little. Unto the Count he said:
   "I love thee not. This judgment through thee is on my
head.
Just Emperor, thou seëst here have I come to thee.
To accomplish thy commandment whatsoever it may be."

XXVI. The Emperor to Ganelon gave o'er his right-hand
glove,
But for the pass in which he was the Count had little love,
And when he should have grasped the glove, he let it fall to
ground.
   "Christ God! What evil meaning in the matter may be
found?
We shall have loss of this embassy," said all the Franks
around.
   "My lords," said Ganelon the Count, "Of this matter ye shall
know."

XXVII. And "Sire," he said to the Emperor, "now give me
leave to go.
Since go I must it were not just here in delay to pine."
   Then said King Charlemagne: "Go forth for Christ his
sake and mine."
With his right hand he absolved him, and crossed him
straight thereon.
Letter and stave forthwith he gave to the Count Ganelon.

XXVIII. Unto his hall went Ganelon. In coat of mail
complete
He armed him, and the golden spurs he buckled on his feet,
And Murglas, the great warsword, he belted at his side.
On Tachebrun the charger he mounted him to ride.
And Guinemer his uncle forth to hold the stirrup stepped.
There might you see good store of knights, despairingly that
wept.
And they said:
                "How evil, Baron, is the lot fallen on thee!
At the King's court well wast thou known a nobleman to be.
And he who wrought that thou shouldst go unto the King of
Spain
Shall not be guarded well enough by the hands of Charle-
magne.

Naught it behoved Count Roland such a matter to begin,
For thou dost trace thy lineage unto a mighty kin."
    After they said: "Now into Spain we pray thee lead us on."
"It were not pleasing in God's sight," gave answer
Ganelon.
"'Twere better I should perish than in the overthrow
My lads should fall. My barons, to sweet France shall ye go.
Give ye my salutation unto my lady dear,
And likewise unto Pinabel who is my friend and peer,
And unto my son Baldwin. Give him your service strong.
Take him for lord."
                        Forth on his way Ganelon rode along.

XXIX. Count Ganelon hath galloped under an olive tall.
The Saracen embassadors were come there one and all.
And Blanchandrin had tarried to await him there the while.
They spoke unto each other in wisdom and in guile.
Said Blanchandrin:
                    "Most marvellous is this man Charlemagne.
He hath conquered all Apulia and the Calabrian Plain.
He hath passed into England over the fair salt sea.
To the profit of Saint Peter he hath ta'en their tribute fee.
What seeks this man among us within the March of Spain?"
    Said the Count:
                    "His lust! Is no man but will fight with him
in vain."

XXX. Said the Paynim:
                    "Gentle are the Franks; but the counts
and dukes do ill
Unto their lord, who give him so bad a counsel still,
For he and many others will perish in the war."
    Said the Count:
                    "Nay, none but Roland; and he shall
smart therefor.
The King sat yestermorning in the shadow of a tree,
And thither came his nephew. In his hauberk clad was he,
For he had been a-raiding by Carcassone in the land.
And a vermilion apple he carried in his hand.
    'Take it, fair Sire,' said Roland unto his uncle then,
'I will give to thee the coronets of all the kings of men.'
His own pride will destroy him. He is given to death each
day.
We would have peace, if any should hap the man to slay."

XXXI. Said Blanchandrin:

        "This Roland is an evil man withal,
That of so many nations would make cowards of them all,
And their governance, moreover, put to hazard in the fight.
How shall he win this glory and by what nation's might?"
  And Ganelon made answer:

        "The Franks shall compass it.
They love him so that never will they fail the man a whit.
Overmuch gold and silver hath Roland given the host,
And mules and steeds and precious cloths and robes of
mighty cost.
And by Count Roland's valor, King Charles his realm hath
won.
And Roland will win the world for him from here to the
rising sun."

XXXII. Count Ganelon and the Paynim rode so far along
the way
That they struck their faith together that Roland they might
slay.
So hard they rode together the roads and highways through
That at last in Saragossa they lighted under a yew.
There was fashioned a high-seat in the shadow of a pine,
Draped in an Alexandrian cloth, most fair that was and fine.
There sat the King that held all Spain, the whole realm far
and wide,
By twenty thousand Saracens girt round on every side.
Not a sound was there. So eager were those about the King
For the tidings that Count Ganelon and Blanchandrin should
bring.

XXXIII. Then Blanchandrin stepped forward before the
King to stand;
And Ganelon beside him, he led him by the hand.
And he said to the King:

        "May now our gods keep thee both safe and sound
Whose holy laws we keep alway—Apollo and Mahound.
We gave thy charge to Charlemagne that raised his hands in
air,
Praising his God, but answer beside he gave none there.
But to thee a noble baron of his henchmen doth he send,
A man of France. Moreover he hath honors without end.
To him now shalt thou hearken if we have peace or none."

Marsile the King gave answer: "We hear. Let him speak
on."

XXXIV. Now Ganelon had thought thereof and his tale
began to tell
Wisely, as a man who knoweth how to shape his dealings well.
He said to the King:
　　　　　　　　"Now swiftly may God's blessing light on thee,
The Glorious, whose servants we evermore should be.
For this is the commandment of the Lord Charlemagne:
That thou become a Christian. Of half the land of Spain
Will he seize thee. Roland master of the rest will he declare.
Thou wilt have a proud co-partner thy provinces to share.
If thou canst not accord thee with the good terms of my King,
His leaguer round Saragossa he certainly will bring.
Thou shalt be bound and captive in the triumph of his power.
To Aix, unto the high-seat will they lead thee in that hour.
Then shall his condemnation end the glory of thy name.
There shalt thou die assuredly in villainy and shame."
Then was King Marsile mastered with terror manifold.
Forthwith he seized the javelin that was wrought with yellow
gold,
And had cast but that his henchmen upon him laid their hold.

XXXV. Changed Marsile's color. In his hand the spear
trembled and swayed.
When Ganelon had seen it he laid hold upon his blade.
To length of his two fingers he laid the weapon bare.
And he said unto the sword-blade:
　　　　　　　　　　　"How clear thou art and fair!
What though I might have worn thee at the court before this
King,
Ne'er shall the Emperor of France of me say such a thing,
That alone I was defeated within the strange countrie.
Ere that the best of them shall buy their dearest blood of
thee."

XXXVI. So hard the greatest Paynims besought the King
of Spain
That Marsile in the high-seat seated himself again.
Forthwith spake out the Algalif:
　　　　　　　　　　　"Thou hast done us all much ill,
Who would have smitten the Frenchman. Thou shouldst
hearken and be still."

Said Ganelon:
        "Lord, with my place to suffer well may stand.
Yet not for all the gold that God hath fashioned by his hand
To say would I give over, if my leisure be so long,
What command to me was given by King Charlemagne the strong,
That it I might deliver to his mortal enemy."
    Ganelon on his shoulders a sable cloak had he.
And a cloth of Alexandria about the cloak was wound.
He cast it off, and Blanchandrin lifted it from the ground.
But to give up the great warsword he would not give accord.
He set his right hand forthwith on the gold hilt of the sword.
Thereupon said the heathen: "This is a gallant lord."

XXXVII. Then unto the King Marsile Count Ganelon drew near
And he said to the King:
        "'Tis ill beseen that thus thou ragest here.
For this is the word of Charles the King that over France
doth reign,
That thou become a Christian. And half the land of Spain
Will he give thee. Roland his nephew with the rest shall be
endowed.
Verily a co-partner thou wilt have exceeding proud.
If thou canst not accord thee with the good terms of my King,
His leaguer round Saragossa he certainly will bring.
Thou shalt be bound and captive in the triumph of his power.
Forthwith to Aix his city will they lead thee in that hour.
Palfrey or battle-charger thou shalt not ride that day.
Mule or she-mule thou shalt not have to gallop on the way.
Upon some evil sumpter-beast thou shalt be thrown instead.
When forth is gone the judgment, then shalt thou lose thine
head.
In the letter that he sendeth our Emperor greets thee fair."
    In his right hand he reached it unto the heathen there.

XXXVIII. The face of Marsile reddened as flashed his
anger out.
He broke the seal in pieces and hurled the wax about.
He looked upon the letter and read it through amain:
    "Lo, what King Charles commands me, that over
France doth reign,
That I should now remember his anger and his pain.
Of Basil and of Basan, he taketh now account
Whereof the heads I severed under Haltilie the mount.

If the life of my dear body I desire to redeem,
Then must I send unto him the Algalif mine eme.
Otherwise in no manner peace with me can he make."
   Thereafter to his father the son of Marsile spake,
And said to the King:
              "Great folly saith Ganelon thee before,
Such folly it were right and meet that he should live no more.
Let me have him to avenge thee."
                  When the Count heard, in air
He brandished blade, and set his back against a pine-trunk
there.

XXXIX. The King into the orchard departed there and then,
And forthwith gathered to him the best of all his men.
And Blanchandrin, moreover, with the white beard came
there,
And also the Prince Jorfaleu, King Marsile's son and heir,
And the King's eme, the Algalif, his faithful man and leal.
   Said Blanchandrin: "Call here the Frank. He hath
sworn to work our weal."
   Said the King: "Do thou then bring him." By the
fingers of his hand
Through the orchard Blanchandrin led him to where the
King did stand.
And there that wicked treason the three contrived and
planned.

XL. "Lo, now, thou good Lord Ganelon," said Marsilies the
King,
"Hereof there is no question; I have wronged thee in this
thing
When in wrath I strove to strike thee, grievously did I err.
Take thou for mine atonement this cloak of marten fur."
More than an hundred golden pounds is worth that minever.
   And Ganelon gave answer:
                   "To this I yield accord.
May God, if it be his pleasure, give thee a great reward."

XLI. "Count Ganelon," said Marsile, "the truth to thee I
tell.
I have it in my spirit to love thee passing well.
I would hear thee speak of Charlemagne, who is old, and
whose day is o'er;

Of years unto my thinking he hath lived a full ten-score.
And he hath borne him manful in many a foreign field,
And many a stroke, moreover, hath taken on his shield;
And of many a wealthy ruler a beggar hath he made.
When will he grow a-weary of the ravage and the raid?"
    "Not such an one is Charlemagne," Ganelon answer gave,
"No man that sees and knows him but knows that he is
brave.
I know not how to praise him or to boast within this place
How much more hath the Emperor of glory and of grace.
What man his deeds of valor is able to relate?
With such a knighthood also our God hath made him great
That better 'twere to perish than to fall from that estate."

XLII. Said the Paynim:
                            "Very greatly I marvel on this score.
This Charlemagne the Emperor is very old and hoar,
After my deeming certainly two hundred years and more.
Such labor of the body hath he wrought in many a land,
Such bitter strokes hath suffered of the battle-spear and
brand,
And of so many rulers poor beggars hath he made.
When will he grow a-weary of the ravage and the raid?"
    "That will not be," said Ganelon, "while Roland's head is
high.
There is not such a vassal neath the hollow of the sky
And a gallant soldier also is his comrade Olivier,
And the twelve peers, moreover, whom Charlemagne holds
dear,
Of twenty thousand horsemen are ever more the van.
Sure is the King among them is not one caitiff man."

XLIII. Said the Paynim:
                            "A great marvel this matter do I
hold,
That Charlemagne the Emperor is grown so white and old.
I deem that more than ten good score of years the man hath
told.
Throughout so many nations he hath conquered near and
far,
So many strokes hath suffered from the keen sword of war,
So many wealthy sovereigns hath he happed to take or
slay.

When then will he be weary of warring thus alway?"
   "That will not be while Roland lives," said the Count
Ganelon,
"There is not such a vassal from here to the rising sun.
And Olivier his comrade is a soldier stark and bold.
And the twelve peers, moreover, that dear the King doth
hold,
Are the vanguard of an army of twenty thousand Franks.
The King knows well no coward is found among their ranks."

XLIV. Marsile the King to Ganelon again the word said he:
"So fair is this my knighthood better is not to see.
Four hundred thousand horsemen are in this host of mine.
Lightly can I fight with Charlemagne and the French battle-
line."
And Ganelon gave answer:
                              "Fight thou not in this hour.
Thou shalt gain a mighty slaughter of all the Paynim power.
But put aside this folly and a wise counsel take:
Out of thy rich possession such a present shalt thou make
To the Emperor that no Frank shall be but shall marvel with-
out end.
And because of the twenty hostages that to him thou shalt
send
Again to the sweet realm of France the Emperor shall repair.
And the rear-guard of the army he shall leave behind him
there.
And then his nephew Roland will be marching with the rear.
And that courteous soldier also, the courageous Olivier.
Dead are the Counts if haply my counsel thou wilt hear.
Charles shall behold his mighty pride how greatly it shall fall.
Further desire for battle he shall not have at all."

XLV. "Prithee, my good Lord Ganelon," did the King
Marsile say,
"In what fashion shall I labor Roland the Count to slay?"
   And Ganelon gave answer:
                              "I will even tell it to thee.
At Sizré in the great defile the Emperor will be,
And his rear-guard behind him to its post he will command.
There will be Roland his nephew that hath so strong an hand,
And Olivier, moreover, whom the King trusteth so.
And twenty thousand Frenchmen in their company will go.

An hundred thousand Paynims thither shalt thou bid fare.
A battle to the Frenchmen they first shall offer there.
Ah, white the faces of the Franks! slaughtered shall be their host,
Not but in lives of soldiers thou shalt bear a mighty cost.
Once more on them in battle in like fashion shalt thou fall;
In which Count Roland perishes it matters not at all.
But thou shalt have done in battle a deed of gentle might,
Nor ever in thy lifetime shalt have need to fight the fight.

XLVI. "Who bringeth to pass that Roland in battle shall be slain,
The right arm of his body shall tear from Charlemagne.
Quiet shall be forever the marvellous hosts of war,
And he will never gather such mighty armies more.
The Greater Land, moreover, in peace and rest shall be."
    When Marsile heard, upon the neck he kissed him eagerly,
And forthwith unto Ganelon let ope his treasury.

XLVII. Again spake the King Marsile:
                        "Why do I not speak forth?
If we be not certain, each of each, the counsel is no worth.
Swear now unto this treason, if faith in thee there be."
And Ganelon gave answer: "It shall fall as pleaseth thee."
    He swore upon the relics in the sword Murglas' hilt
To carry out the treason. Thus was compassed all his guilt.

XLVIII. Thereby there stood a high-seat wrought out of elephant horn.
King Marsile let before him a certain book be borne.
Mahound and Termagaunt their law therein was written plain.
And then his oath upon it sware that Saracen of Spain
That, if upon Count Roland in the rear-guard he might light,
With the whole array of Paynims against him would he smite;
And, were it his lot, would perish like a true man in the fray.
    Said Ganelon: "Now blessings on our covenant alway."

XLIX. Then laughing clear strode forward a Paynim Valda-bron,
And raised up the King Marsile, and spake to Ganelon:
    "Take now my sword. A better no man at all hath found,

Only the hilt of the great sword is worth a thousand pound.
Out of pure love and friendship I give it to thee here.
By thee shall we find Count Roland in the army of the rear."
    Then answered the Count Ganelon: "Right shall be done herein."
Thereon they kissed each other on the cheek and on the chin.

L. And Climborin a Paynim came forward at a stride,
And clearly rang his laughter as to Ganelon he cried:
    "Take now my helm. In no place have I seen a better helm.
Through thee the Marquis Roland in dishonor shall we whelm."
    Thereon said Ganelon the Count: "Herein shall right be done."
Forthwith they kissed each other the cheek and lip upon.

LI. Then to the place came Bramimonde (King Marsile's queen was she)
She said unto Count Ganelon:
                              "I greatly honor thee.
My lord esteems thee greatly, and all his men beside.
Behold, fair Sire, these bracelets will I send unto thy bride.
With amethyst and jacinth and gold they are fashioned well,
And more than all the treasure are they worth that Rome can tell.
Jewels of such rich excellence thine Emperor hath none."
    The gems into his riding boots thrust the Count Ganelon.

LII. Said the King unto his treasurer: "Dight is the Emperor's gift?"
    "Yea, Sire," the man gave answer, "it is well enough to shift.
Seven hundred camels laden with silver and gold are by,
And likewise twenty hostages the gentlest under sky."

LIII. On the shoulder of Count Ganelon, King Marsile laid his hand.
He said:
          "Thou art very gallant and quick to understand.
By that law which for holiest thou holdest in thy heart,
Keep thee well that in no manner thou shalt falter from our part.

Good store of my possessions will I give o'er to thee.
I will load ten mules with the finest of the gold of Araby.
No year shall pass but to thee a like present I will make.
And the keys of this great city I prithee now to take.
Give thou to Charles the Emperor these gifts of mighty cost.
Then bring it to pass that Roland in the rear shall have his
post.
If in the mountain passes upon him I shall light,
The battle that I offer shall be a mortal fight."
    And Ganelon gave answer: "Too long do I delay."
He mounted on his charger and galloped on his way.

LIV. Again the Emperor Charlemagne drew nigh unto his
home.
To the town of Valtierra in that hour was he come.
Roland the Count that city had overthrown and ta'en.
After that day an hundred years a waste did it remain.
For tidings of Count Ganelon a space abode the King,
And the great Spanish Empire her splendid ransoming.
And at the crack of day-break, when the clear morning
glowed,
Into the King's encampment Count Ganelon he rode.

LV. Betimes upon that morning the King himself bestirred,
And Mass and Matin Service already had he heard.
He sat by his pavilion upon the grass so green.
Roland and the brave Olivier beside him there were seen.
Duke Neimes there stood by them, and many another chief.
And thither came Count Ganelon the traitor and the thief.
Forthwith he 'gan a-talking in his wicked treachery.
    "God's blessing be upon thee," unto the King said he.
"The keys of Saragossa unto thee I have brought.
Besides them I am charged for thee with a treasure richly
fraught,
And a score of hostages as well. Do thou keep them close in
hand.
Marsile the brave beseeches concerning thy demand
In the matter of the Algalif, blame not the Saracen.
With mine own eyes did I behold four hundred thousand men
That all wore iron helmets and all were hauberk-clad,
And girded at their girdles gold-pointed swords that had.
They marched beside the Algalif to the margin of the sea,
Whither they fled because of dread of our Christianity,

Which they had no desire to receive or to maintain.
Scarce four leagues had they sailed, when burst the stormy
hurricane.
There were they drowned, and never more that army shalt
thou see.
If the Algalif were living I had brought him here with me.
Hear thou tidings of the Paynim. This month shall not have
sped
Ere into France the kingdom in thy footsteps he will tread.
There will he take thy faith on him with meetly folded hands.
Thee will he serve, and hold in fief of thee the Spanish lands."
   "Now to my God be glory," said the King Charlemagne,
"Well hast thou wrought the service, and great shall be thy gain."
Amid that host together did a thousand trumpets bray.
They broke their camp. The sumpter-beasts they loaded on
that day,
And home to the sweet realm of France the army took the
way.

LVI. The whole of Spain King Charlemagne had wasted and
had wracked;
The castles he had taken, and the cities he had sacked.
But now the time of battle, he said was past and o'er,
And back to the sweet realm of France he wended from the
war.
On a spear the army's ensign Count Roland carried high:
On the summit of a little hill he raised it to the sky.
The Franks made their encampment o'er the whole country-
side.
But along through the wide valley the Paynim army hied.
In hauberk and double byrnie, with laced helm on the head,
Sword by side, shield on shoulder, and lance in hand they
sped.
On the summit of the mountains in a wood abided they.
Four hundred thousand waited for the breaking of the day.
God! What a woe! The Frenchmen deem little of that ill.

LVII. At length the day passed over and the night was calm
and still.
Then fell asleep the Emperor, the powerful and great.
He dreamed at Sizré that he was, in the huge mountain gate,
And in his hands he carried his spear with the ashen heft,
And from his hand Count Ganelon the mighty weapon reft.
With such a savage fury he shook and brandished it

That the splinters flew to heaven. Yet the King waked no
whit.

LVIII. And after this first vision another dream he dreamed.
In France in his own chapel in the town of Aix he seemed.
And a bear bit his right shoulder, that was furious and fell.
And he saw out of Arden a leopard come as well,
That fierily assailed him. Then quickly to the King
There galloped a good greyhound with many a bound and
spring.
The right ear of the mighty bear first with its teeth it caught.
And a battle with the leopard the gallant greyhound fought.
And the Franks spake of the greatness of the battle in the
hall,
And none might know to which of them the victory would
fall.
And the Emperor slept ever, nor wakened then at all.

LIX. At length the night passed over. White broke the morn-
ing sky.
Proud rode the King, and the war-horns through the army
sounded high.
    "Lord barons," said King Charlemagne, "the mountain
pass ye see.
Say which chief of the army in the rear-guard shall be."
    "Lo! Roland that is my stepson," gave answer Ganelon,
"A baron of such following in the whole host hast thou none."
    And the King looked upon him and angry was his brow,
And he said unto Count Ganelon:
                                "A devil alive art thou.
And mortal rage and anger to thy heart has entered in.
With the vanguard of my army shall march what paladin?"
    Said Ganelon:
                        "Then Ogier of Denmark let it be.
None hast thou that the matter may speed so well as he."

LX. And thereupon Count Roland when the judgment he did
hear
Spake forth to them his counsel like a good cavalier:
    "Lord stepfather, much kindness now unto thee I owe,
That the ruling of the rear-guard hast brought upon me so.
King Charles that holds the realm of France shall never lose
indeed,
After my understanding, palfrey, or battle steed.

He shall lose no mule nor she-mule whereon a man may ride,
Nor any packhorse either, nor sumpter-beast beside,
Wherefor the sword in battle hath not made a purchase fell."
     And Ganelon gave answer: "Truth say'st thou I know
well."

LXI. When with the rear-guard he should go that the Count
Roland heard,
Then unto his stepfather he spoke a bitter word:
     "Thou traitor! thou most wicked! born of a shameful line!
Thou thinkest here the glove will fall out of this hand of mine,
Even as the staff of office fell erewhile out of thine."

LXII. Count Roland to King Charlemagne his voice uplifted
there.
     "Give me the bow that in thy hand thou evermore dost
bear.
That no man shall reproach me that I dropped it, I deem well,
As, when Ganelon took the truncheon, with thy right glove
it befell."
     The Emperor bent down his brow when spoke the paladin;
Aye plucked he with his fingers at the beard on lip and chin;
And the tears that came into his eyes, he could not keep them
in.

LXIII. Neimes stood forth thereafter. And there was not to
see
In all the court a vassal that was better man than he.
He said unto the Emperor:
                         "Well the matter hast thou heard.
The anger of Count Roland is very greatly stirred.
His is the rear. No baron in his place may well command.
The bow which thou hast offered give now into his hand.
And whoso'er will aid him now seek thou high and low."
     And the King gave it over, and Roland took the bow.

LXIV. The Emperor called Roland. "Lord Nephew," then
said he,
"Know truly, half mine army will I leave now with thee.
Do thou keep them for thy safety." Said the Count:
                                        "Nay, Sire, the thing
I will not do. God slay me if my line to shame I bring

Twenty thousand gallant Frenchmen will I keep. The gate-
way here
Safe shalt thou pass, nor while I live for any shalt thou fear."

LXV. Upon his steed of battle the good Count Roland got.
And Olivier his comrade came to him at the spot,
And Gerin was come thither, and Count Gerier the strong;
And thither also Berenger and Othon came along;
And there did Anseïs the proud, and Samson too appear;
And Ivoris and Ivo, whom the King held so dear.
Gerard of Roussillon was there; an ancient man was he;
And Engelier, moreover, of the land of Gascony.
Quoth Turpin the Archbishop: "I will go too, by my head."
   "And I with thee," Count Walter to the Archbishop said,
"For I am Roland's liegeman. By him I must abide."
   Knights were there twenty thousand that thus came forth
beside.

LXVI. To Walter-a-Hume Count Roland has given his
command:
   "Take now a thousand Franks with thee that are come of
France our land.
And prithee get the passes and the little hills in hand,
Lest by ill hap the Emperor should suffer loss thereby."
"It is my bounden duty," said Walter in reply.
Therewith he led his squadrons to seize the pass on high.
But he will not come down again (for ill news flies about)
Before swords seven hundred to battle are drawn out.
King Almaris that in Belferne the kingdom held his sway
The most terrible of battles will fight with him that day.

LXVII. High were the peaks about them, and dark the vale
and black,
Sombre the rocks around them, and terrible the track.
All day the French were marching in labor and in pain.
For fifteen leagues the bruit a man might hear it plain.
But when they came to the Greater Land and Gascony
discerned,
Even their King's own country, then the memory returned
Of fiefs and farms and children and their gentle wives and
good.
Was no man but for pity was weeping where he stood.

But greater than any other's was the grief of Charlemagne
That he had left his nephew within the Gate of Spain.
And he wept for very pity, for all he was not fain.

LXVIII. In Spain abode the twelve good peers, with twenty
thousand by
Of Franks that felt no fear at all and dreaded not to die,
King Charlemagne the Emperor hied onward into France;
But underneath his mantle he hid his countenance.
Neimes rode near: "What thinkest thou? he said unto the
King.
    Charles said:
                "He doth me bitter wrong that asketh me this
thing.
I have so sore a sorrow, what can I do but moan?
By Ganelon the land of France is wrecked and overthrown.
Yesternight in a vision an angel showed me clear
How in my hands Count Ganelon had splintered all my spear,
Even he that wrought this matter so that Roland took the
rear.
And I have left him lonely in a strange land behind.
God's name, if I should lose him his like I shall not find."

LXIX. King Charles the mighty Emperor wept, for all he
was not fain.
For him a hundred thousand Franks suffered great grief and
pain.
And for the good Count Roland great fear they had as well.
Count Ganelon the traitor had wrought that treason fell.
From the sovereign of the Saracens resplendent gifts had he,
Gold and silver and noble cloths, and silken finery,
And of lions, steeds and camels and mules great company.
King Marsile bade his barons come unto him amain,
Counts, viscounts, dukes, and almaçors of the fair land of
Spain
With the emirs and the children of the counts throughout the
land.
And full four hundred thousand were added to his hand.
The drums in Saragossa he bade beat them in that hour.
They carried up Mahomet into the highest tower.
Thereby was found no Paynim but did worship and adore.
Then out with a great tumult the army rode to war.
Through Cerdagne, and through the valleys and the moun-

tains they marched on,
Until of the French army they saw the gonfalon,
Where all the twelve companions with the French rear-guard
lay.
King Marsile will not tarry till he has joined the fray.

LXX. The nephew of King Marsile before them all did stand.
He smote the mule he rode on with the cudgel in his hand.
In merriment his uncle right fairly he bespake:
    "Fair Lord and King, much service have I compassed for
thy sake.
Much have I suffered for thee in labor and in pain.
I have fought many a battle and won the field amain.
To fight this fight with Roland, now give me guerdon here;
And I myself will slay him with the sharp point of the spear.
If that Mahomet unto me his favor fair will grant,
I will free all Spain from the Aspre pass even to Durestant.
Charlemagne shall be weary, and the Franks shall be sick of
war.
Thou shalt never have a battle in all thy lifetime more."
    To his nephew the King Marsile forthwith the glove gave
o'er.

LXXI. The nephew of King Marsile in his hand the glove did
take.
And there unto his uncle a fiery word he spake:
    "My fair Lord King, a mighty thing hast thou given unto
me.
Choose now eleven barons out of thy chivalry.
Against the twelve companions to battle will I ride."
    And first of all one Falsaron gave answer and replied
(He was King Marsile's brother): "Nephew, let us away,
For thou and I together shall surely fight this fray.
The rear-guard of the gallant host that Charles to battle led,
Surely the thing is written that we shall strike them dead."

LXXII. King Corsablis, moreover, rose up upon his part.
From the land of Barbary was he, a man of wicked art.
He spake like a good vassal in the law of chivalry,
And not for all the gold of God a coward would he be.
And Malprimis of Brigal, behold, came running there.
On his feet was he faster than any steed to fare.
With a loud voice to Marsile his purpose he did show:

"I will adventure my body in the pass of Roncevaux.
And if I come on Roland, he shall get his overthrow."

LXXIII. An admiral, moreover, of Balaguer was there.
Most splendid was his body, and his face was proud and fair.
Gallant he was to ride in arms and to gallop on his steed.
And for great feats of battle men gave him aye his meed.
Had he been Christian, noble had he been in very deed.
And he cried before King Marsile:
                                    "I will ride in Roncevaux.
If I may come on Roland, I will bring his head full low.
To the twelve peers and Olivier I will even do the same.
All of the French shall perish in sorrow and in shame.
Old and weak in understanding is the Emperor Charlemagne.
He will dread sore the battle to undertake again.
In liberty shall Spain abide to us forevermore."
     And the King Marsile forthwith thanked him right well
therefor.

LXXIV. An almaçor of Moriane before the King did stand.
There was no greater scoundrel in all the Spanish land.
And he made his boast.
                       "To Roncevaux with my men will I advance.
There be full twenty thousand with buckler and with lance.
I swear, an I come on Roland, by my hand he shall be slain.
No day shall pass but the sorrow shall weigh on Charle-
magne."

LXXV. Turgis of Tortelosa rose also at that tide.
He was a count, and the city was his heritage beside.
He hated well the Christians. To the others by the King
He strode and said to Marsile:
                               "Fear thou not anything.
For greater than Saint Peter, the Roman, is Mahound.
If thou serve him, to our honor the victory shall redound.
I will ride forth with Roland in Roncevaux to fight.
There is no man shall save him from death and from despite.
Seest thou my long and splendid blade. 'Gainst the edge of
Durendal
Will I set it. Swiftly shalt thou hear how victory shall fall.
The French are dead, an we find them. Sorrow and ill renown
Shall come to Charles the ancient that no more shall wear the
crown."

LXXVI. Escremis of Valtierra before them all did stand.
He was a Saracen indeed: and his was all that land.
And unto the King Marsile right through the press he cried:
  "I too will go to Roncevaux to overthrow their pride.
If I come on the Count Roland, there shall he lose his head,
And likewise the Lord Olivier who ruleth in his stead.
The twelve are doomed to perish. The French shall all be slain.
France shall lie waste. Good vassals shall be lost to Charle-magne."

LXXVII. And Estorgant a Paynim before them did appear,
And Estramaris, moreover, his boon companion dear.
There were no falser traitors nor felons in the land.
To them cried out King Marsile:
                        "Now forth before us stand.
Unto the Gates of Roncevaux, ye two shall get you gone.
There shall ye aid my marshals to lead mine army on."
  And they answered
                "O King Marsile we wait on thy command.
Against Olivier and Roland we twain will lift the hand.
The peers will have no warrant that death they may with-stand.
Behold our blades of battle that are so keen and good.
Vermilion will we make them with the hot bursts of blood.
The French shall perish. Charlemagne in sorrow shall be bent.
The Greater Land for a good gift to thee we shall present.
Come there, O King, if that the thing thou verily wouldst see.
The Emperor we will give o'er for a suppliant to thee."

LXXVIII. Then Margaris of Seville came running there beside.
His land unto the sea-coast extended far and wide.
And all the ladies loved him for his fair countenance.
None ever lived that saw him but brightened at the glance,
And, would she not or would she, from smiling could forbear.
So chivalrous a gallant was no other Paynim there.
He came amid the others and shouted through the press,
And he said unto King Marsile:
                        "Have no manner of distress.
I will go unto Roncevaux. Count Roland will I slay.
Neither shall the Lord Olivier carry his life away.
And the twelve peers, moreover, hard death shall have and hold.

Look now unto my weapon with the great hilt of gold.
The Admiral of Prime that sword gave for a gift to me,
And drenched in the vermilion blood I promise it shall be.
And all the French shall perish, and France be shamed in that hour.
And Charlemagne the ancient, with the great beard like a flower,
Shall never have a day go by, but woe and wrath shall betide.
Let but a year pass over we shall have all France beside.
In the city of Saint Denis at our ease we then may lie."
    The master of the Paynims bowed his head low in reply.

LXXIX. Cornubel of the Black Valley stood forth from those around,
And his long hair about him swept down unto the ground.
He bore a greater burden for a jest, when he would play
Than seven mules could carry. In the country, so they say,
That he came from is no sunshine, nor groweth any grain,
Nor is there any dew at all nor any falling rain.
And the stones in that country they are all black as well.
And men say this, moreover, that there the devils dwell.
    "My good sword have I girded," then Cornubel he said,
"When I brandish it at Roncevaux I wot it shall be red.
If I come on that proud Roland in the middle of my way,
If I attack not, let no man believe me from that day.
There Durendal will I conquer with this good sword of mine own.
There all the French shall perish and France be overthrown!"
    At that word the twelve companions on their way rode along.
Of Saracens they led with them an hundred thousand strong,
That were eager for the battle and hasted on the way.
And underneath a pine-wood they armed them for the fray.

LXXX. In the strong hauberks Saracen, themselves the Paynims clad.
The greater number armor of triple thickness had.
Good helms of Saragossa they laced upon them then,
And they girded swords upon them of the sharp steel of Vienne.
They held Valentian lances, and shield on shoulder wore.
White and blue and vermilion were the gonfalons they bore.
Behind they left the palfreys and the sumpter mules to stray.

They mounted on the chargers and rode in close array.
The sun broke on them splendid, and fair the morning came;
There was no bit of armor but was blazing in a flame;
And to make it yet more glorious a thousand horns blew clear.
So mighty was the uproar that the French at last did hear.
   Said Olivier:
               "My comrades, and my good lords I trow
With the Saracens a battle we are like to have one now."
   Count Roland spake in answer:
                    "Now may God grant the thing.
Well now should ever man of us bestir him for our King.
That for his overlord a man should suffer much is meet.
He should risk for him both life and limb and bear both cold
and heat.
Let every man look to it that he strike good strokes and
strong;
Never of any man of us shall they sing an evil song.
For wrong is with the Paynims, but with the Christians
right.
Never an ill example will I set you in the fight."

LXXXI. Over the mountain ridges Olivier climbed on high.
And down a grassy valley on the right he cast his eye,
And saw the Paynim army how hard on them it hied.
Then to his comrade Roland with a loud voice he cried:
   "There cometh a great press of men out of the land of
Spain—
A host of the white hauberks. The helmets flash again.
They shall stir up in our Frenchmen a great wrath fierce and
fell.
Count Ganelon the traitor hath wrought his treason well,
He who before the Emperor this judgment did decide."
   "Peace, Olivier," unto him Roland the Count replied.
"'Tis my stepfather. I like not that thou speak of him so."

LXXXII. Over the peak Lord Olivier now hasted him to go.
Out and across the realm of Spain an eager look he threw,
And he beheld the Paynim host that there together drew.
And from their gold-wrought helmets a blazing light did
dance
On shield and broidered hauberk, on pennant and on lance.
Not even might he number the battalions of the foe.
There were so many of them their strength he could not know.

Within him was he troubled. He hastened as he might
From the hill and told the Frenchmen all the terror of that
sight.

LXXXIII. "I have looked upon the Paynims," Lord Olivier
said he;
"There is no man upon the earth that a greater host shall see.
Under shield an hundred thousand in the van alone do fare
That are clad in milk-white hauberks, and well-laced helms
that wear.
Straight are the spear-shafts, glittering are the brown spears
of war.
Ye are like to have such a battle as was never fought before.
Lord Franks of God take courage that we be not beaten this
day."
    Said the Franks:
              "God's shame upon him that runneth hence away.
For fear of death not one of us shall fail thee or betray."

LXXXIV. Said Olivier:
                  "The Paynims a mighty army lead.
But our good Franks meseemeth are few in very deed.
Oh my good comrade Roland, blow on thy horn amain.
And Charlemagne shall hear it and come with the host again."
    And Roland gave his answer:
                    "I should be as a fool forlorn;
In France should I lose mine honor, if I blew upon my horn
For the Paynims; but with Durendal the great strokes will I
deal.
Up to the golden sword-hilt the blood shall stain the steel.
To the rock-defiles, fell Paynims, ye come in evil hour.
Now unto death, I swear it, is given all your power."

LXXXV. "Oh my Companion Roland, blow on thy horn
amain.
King Charles the Great will hear it and come with the host
again.
And the King shall bear us succor, and with him many a
knight."
    And Roland answered:
                   "Never were it pleasing in God's
sight
That ever men my parents because of me should blame,

Or ever the sweet realm of France should come on bitter
shame.
I will do enow with Durendal the sword at my side so good.
Ye shall see the brand within my hand made ruddy with the
blood.
Fell Paynims in an evil hour are ye gathered. On my faith
The whole of your great battle shall be given unto death."

LXXXVI. "Oh my good comrade Roland, but blow thy horn
the while,
King Charlemagne shall hear it on his march in the defile."
   "It were not pleasing unto God," did Roland answer give,
"That such a thing should e'er be said of any that doth live.
That because of any Paynim the war-horn I have blown.
Never upon my parents shall such a smirch be thrown.
And when at last I gallop in the gigantic fight,
A thousand and seven hundred of the great strokes will I
smite.
Of Durendal hereafter shall ye see the bloody steel.
The Franks, an it be God's pleasure, shall fight like vassals
leal.
The Paynims bring no warrant against the slaughter here."

LXXXVII. "Herein is found no shame at all," gave answer
Olivier.
"Nay but the Saracens of Spain. I have seen their battle
clear,
And the valley and the mountain and the moorland and the
plain
With the great host of the stranger are covered up amain.
And all of us together but a little host are we."
   And Roland made him answer:
                                   "The fiercer will I be.
God and the Holy Angels would deem it an ill day,
If France should lose her honor when Roland feared the fray.
Better it were to perish than that shame on us should light.
King Charles will hold us dearer the stronglier that we smite."

LXXXVIII. Proud is the Marquis Roland and Olivier is wise.
The twain of them, moreover, are men of gallant guise.
When they are mounted on the steed and have got their
harness on,
Then never though they perish the battle will they shun.

Both of the Counts are gallant, and their words high and free.
   In mighty anger marches the host of heathenry.
   "Roland, look for a little," Lord Olivier did say.
"Behold they are hard upon us and Charles is far away.
A blast upon the war-horn thou wouldst not deign to blow.
Were the King here among us we were not perilled so.
Look up unto the mountain where the Aspre gates appear;
There mayst thou see the sorrow of the army of the rear.
He who so wrought the matter in no other fray shall ride."
   And unto the Lord Olivier Roland the Count replied:
   "So great a shame and folly I prithee speak not thou,
But let him be accursed who turneth coward now.
Within this place together we shall stand against the foes.
Here shall we deal together the buffets and the blows."

LXXXIX. When well had Roland seen it that a battle soon
would be,
Then lordlier than a leopard or a lion stark was he.
He shouted to the Frenchmen and to Olivier he cried:
   "My lord and my companions! now say no more beside.
The Emperor who his Frenchmen hath given to our hand,
Hath left us twenty thousand that here with us shall stand.
That not a man among them is a coward he is sure.
And for his lord great evil a good man must endure,
And bear great heat, moreover, and likewise bitter cold.
And flesh and blood of his body to lose he must be bold.
Smite with the lance. With Durendal the battle will I try,
The good blade the King gave me. And if I hap to die,
He that shall have it hereafter, shall say about the sword
That it was a good vassal's who was faithful to his lord."

XC. There was Archbishop Turpin upon the other hand
He spurred his charger onwards. On a hill he took his stand
And unto all the Frenchmen he spoke a message clear.
   "Lord barons, Charles the Emperor hath left us in the rear.
And for our King and Master behoveth us to die.
Quit you like men for Christendom, that it may stand there-
by.
Ye may be sure and certain that your battle soon will be,
For with your eyes each man of you the Saracens may see.
Do ye forthwith confess your sins; for God his mercy pray.
To save your souls His healing upon you I will lay.
Ye will be holy martyrs, if in the fight ye fall.

In the fair land of Paradise ye shall sit one and all."
   And forthwith did the Frenchmen upon the ground alight,
And kneeled, and the Archbishop he blessed them by God's
might,
And bade them for their penance upon the foe to smite.

XCI. Up rose thereon the Frenchmen. Upon their feet they
got.
Absolved they were and pardoned of their sins upon the spot.
And the Archbishop Turpin hath blessed them by God's
power.
Upon the battle-chargers they mounted in that hour.
They armed them like good champions. They donned their
war-array
And thereupon Count Roland to Olivier did say:
   "Oh, my good lord and comrade, Surely thou saidest well,
And I believe, we are betrayed by Ganelon the fell.
And gold and rich possessions hath the man purchased thus.
The Emperor great vengeance must surely take for us.
To march on us, to Marsile hath Ganelon sent word.
They shall barter now that treason for the edges of the
sword."

XCII. Through the Gates of Spain went Roland on Valiant
the great steed,
With all his armor on him that became him well indeed.
He bore the good spear in his hand with the point unto the
height.
Upon the summit of the spear was laced a pennant white.
About his hands went flashing the fringes of the gold.
His face was fair with laughter and within his heart was bold.
And hard upon his footsteps came his good company,
And the men of France proclaimed him their champion to be.
He cast upon the Saracen a fierce glance and a proud,
But a fair and gentle on the French, and he spake sweet word
aloud:
   "Ride slowly, my lord barons. To their slaughter do they
come.
We shall carry from the Paynim a mighty booty home.
No king of France before us such treasure e'er has ta'en."
Scarce had his words been spoken, when the armies met
amain.

XCIII. Said Olivier to Roland:

> "I will even speak my fill.

The mighty horn of battle to blow thou hadst no will.
Now unto us King Charlemagne no succour can afford;
He knows not of our peril and no blame is to our lord.
And the soldiers of the army we may blame them in no way.
But ride ye like good cavaliers, as fiercely as ye may.
To keep the field, lord barons, now firm your spirits make;
By God I pray you steel yourselves the blows to give and
take.
We will remember ever King Charles his battle-shout."
   And as he finished speaking the Frenchmen roared it out.
Well might he think on loyalty Mountjoy that tide that
heard.
Then they galloped in great glory. At utmost speed they
spurred.
They will smite, (what can they other?) But the foe feared
not the war.
And full against each other the Franks and Paynims bore.

XCIV. Forth rode King Marsile's nephew, (Aldelroth was his
name)
And first of all the army before the host he came.
Concerning our good Frenchmen he spake evil on his way:
   "What ho, ye Frankish villains, ye shall joust with us
this day.
And he who should have saved you has betrayed you to your
fate.
A fool is the King Charlemagne that left you at the gate.
Away from the sweet realm of France her glory shall be ta'en.
And, moreover, from his body the right arm of Charlemagne."
   But God! when Roland heard it, he was filled with wrath
untold.
He pricked the battle charger with the great spurs of gold.
The Count rode in to strike him as fiercely as he might,
He brake the shield; through the hauberk a great stroke did
he smite.
Right through the Paynim's body the weapon good he drave.
The bones he brake in pieces, the chest he cut and clave.
And the strong spine he severed in the back of the cavalier;
The spirit from the body he harried with the spear.
So well he smote that Paynim that he staggered there indeed;
With the swift lance did Roland beat the dead man from the
steed.

And with that stroke he shattered all the knight's neck in
twain;
Yet none the less Count Roland spake forth unto the slain:
  "Get hence, thou slave! no villain is Charlemagne the King.
As for the sin of treason he loveth not the thing.
When he left us in the passes he did as a brave man may.
And not a whit of glory sweet France shall lose to-day.
Strike now, my Franks! Unto us the first stroke doth belong.
We have the right of the battle. These villains have the
wrong."

XCV. A duke was there hight Falsaron. Marsile's brother
was he.
Of Dathan and Abiram he held the land in fee.
Than he a feller villain was not beneath the skies.
Exceeding broad and mighty was his brow between the
eyes—
A full half foot by measure a man might see it spread—
He had his fill of sorrow when he saw his nephew dead.
Through the press with the Paynim war-cry Duke Falsaron
made way
And shouted in his fury: "France shall be shamed this day."
Olivier heard. Within him did mighty anger stir.
He pricked the battle charger with the good golden spur.
Therewith the shield he shattered, and the hauberk all to-
broke.
Through the side the pennant-fringes were driven at the
stroke.
With the swift lance from the arçon he smote the Paynim
dead,
And looked on the villain where he lay, and a proud word
he said:
  "Knave! never for your menace shall I have care again.
Strike Franks into the mellay, and the battle we will gain!"
  And he gave "Mountjoy" the war-cry, the shout of
Charlemagne.

XCVI. There was a king, one Corsablis, that thither came to
hand.
And he was come from Barbary and dwelt in the strange land.
He called to the other Paynims:
                              "Well may we win the day.
The army of the Frenchmen but a little host are they

And those that stand before us we should hold in little dread.
Not one unto King Charlemagne shall carry hence his head.
Now is their time upon them, the hour when they shall die."
    But Turpin the Archbishop, full well he heard the cry.
Was no man under heaven that he did hate so sore.
He pricked the steed with the fair gold spurs, and gallantly he
bore
Against the foe to smite him. The buckler there he clove,
And shivered the hauberk. Through the shield the splendid
lance he drove.
He struck him that he staggered. He smote him dead in the
way
With the lance, and then looked downward to where the
villain lay.
Nor did he cease from bitter speech, but then aloud he cried:
    "Get hence, thou slavish traitor! Full loudly hast thou lied.
My lord King Charles will aid us. Our Franks have no desire
To flee, but thy companions, we will teach them till they tire.
Another death hereafter must thou suffer yet again.
Strike in, strike in, ye Frenchmen! forget not ye are men.
The first stroke cometh on our side; to God the praises be."
    Thereon "Mountjoy!" he shouted for desire of victory.

XCVII. And on Malprimis of Brigal the good lord Gerin
smote.
The great shield that he carried availed him not a groat.
And the fair crystal buckle in pieces small he brast.
The half of the fair buckle down on the ground was cast.
The hauberk he tore asunder, even unto the skin,
Deep, deep into the body he thrust the good lance in.
At the one stroke the heathen upon the ground did roll.
And in that hour Satan hath carried off his soul.

XCVIII. And Gerier his good comrade the Admiral o'er-
threw.
He broke the shield. The hauberk, he rended it in two,
And his good lance, moreover, right through the heart he ran.
He smote so well he drove it through the body of the man.
Dead to the ground with the swift lance the enemy he bore.
    Thereon said the Lord Olivier: "Most gallant is our war."

XCIX. Duke Samson 'gainst the Almaçor rode out to strike
a stroke.

The golden-flowered buckler in pieces there he broke.
His hauberk then that Saracen stood him in stead not well.
Through heart and lungs and liver the sword of Samson fell.
And, would ye not or would ye, he smote the fellow dead.
    "Yon is a baron's sword-stroke," Archbishop Turpin said.

C. And Anseïs thereafter let his war-charger go.
Turgis of Tortelosa he rode to overthrow.
And the great shield he shattered 'neath the buckle of the gold.
Of the hauberk fair, moreover, he burst the double fold.
He struck him through the body with the sharp head of the spear —
So well that on the other side all of the steel was clear.
With the swift lance dead on the field he hurled the heathen down.
    Said Roland: "That was the spear-stroke of a hero of renown."

CI. And Engelier of Bordeaux, the Gascon, came amain.
He spurred the charger onwards, he loosed the bridle-rein.
Escremis of Valtierra he galloped in to slay.
He clove the shield of the Paynim that the cantels fell away.
Out of the heathen hauberk the steel rings did he wrest.
Between the man's two shoulders he stabbed him through the breast.
And dead out of the saddle he hurled him with the spear.
    Thereon aloud he shouted: "Ye all shall perish here!"

CII. And Othon smote a Paynim, and Estorgant he hight.
Upon the forepart of the shield on the leather did he smite,
That he cut away the colors, the vermilion and the white.
The steel plates of the hauberk he rended them and tore.
Right through the Paynim's body the cutting spear he bore.
Down from the running charger he struck the villain dead.
    And he spake: "There was no warrant 'gainst death to stand thy stead."

CIII. And Berenger, moreover, Estramaris smote he;
He broke his shield, he shattered the hauberk utterly.
So through the heart of the Paynim the mighty spear he sped
That amid a thousand Saracens he struck the fellow dead.
Of the twelve peers of the Paynims now ten good men are slain.

Alive of all that fellowship but two of them remain.
And Cornubel and Margaris the Marquis are the twain.

CIV. And Margaris the Marquis was a very stalwart knight.
Stalwart he was and beautiful and swift of foot and light.
Spurring 'gainst Olivier, his way to smite him did he hold.
He shattered all the target 'neath the buckle of pure gold.
Along the flank of the good Frank he thrust the battle-spear.
But by God's aid he hurt not the side of Olivier.
For the great lance but grazed him, nor dealt him any wound,
And Margaris unhindered went beyond him with a bound,
And to summon up his henchmen upon his horn did sound.

CV. Marvellous is the battle and all men fight the fray.
And from it the Count Roland no whit he kept away.
With the lance he fought while in his hand the spear-shaft
did remain.
But fifteen strokes have wrenched it and broken it in twain.
Then forth he drew great Durendal, the naked goodly glaive.
He spurred the steed; to slay him at Cornubel he drave.
He shattered all the helmet where the carbuncles shone fair.
He clave through the white linen cap and through the mighty
hair,
And through his eyes and visage, and through the hauberk
white
With little links, to the forking of the body did he smite.
And right through the rich saddle of beaten gold wrought well,
And the great steed thereunder, the blade of Roland fell.
It broke the back of the charger. Where was no joint did it
pass.
There Roland struck dead Cornubel on the thick growing
grass.
    After he said:
                    "Thou coward, an ill-come man wast thou.
No succor by Mahomet shall be granted to thee now.
And such a very villain shall win no war to-day."

CVI. Count Roland on the charger through the battle made
his way,
And Durendal that cut and thrust so well in hand he bore.
In that hour of those Saracens he made a slaughter sore.
Ah! but to see him hurling the slain upon the slain,
And the clear blood a-flowing that spouted on the plain!

And bloody was his hauberk, and his arms were steeped in
blood.
Red were the neck and shoulders of the charger great and
good.
Upon the Paynims Olivier no whit was slow to fall.
The twelve peers in that battle deserved no blame at all.
And all the French, moreover, came charging on to slay.
There many Paynims perished or in terror swooned away.
Said Turpin then: "Our chivalry like men the fight maintain."
    He cried the great cry of Mountjoy the cry of Charle-
magne.

CVII. Up and through the battle went riding Olivier.
Split was his lance. He carried but a truncheon of the spear.
He rode against a Paynim, and Malsaron he hight.
Through the golden-flowered helmet a great stroke did he
smite.
Both of his eyes from the man's head Lord Olivier did beat.
The brains of the smitten Paynim fell down unto his feet.
With Malsaron he overthrew seven hundred of his men.
And Turgis and Estorgos the twain he slaughtered then.
The lance-haft to his hand-grasp was splintered and to-broke.
    "What dost thou, my companion?" So the Count Roland
spoke,
"In such a bitter battle for a truncheon have no care.
The sharp steel and the iron have richer value there.
Where is the great sword Haulteclair that thou wast wont to
hold,
Whose pommel is of crystal and the great hilt all of gold?"
    And Olivier gave answer: "I could not draw it indeed
To smite within the battle, too eager was my need."

CVIII. And thereupon Lord Olivier the goodly war-sword
drew,
Even as his comrade Roland had besought him so to do,
And like to a good cavalier held it in all men's sight.
On Justin of Val-Ferrée the Paynim did he smite.
And the head of that same Paynim in pieces twain he smote,
And clove him through the body and the embroidered coat.
And right through the good saddle set with fair gold and fine
Swiftly the stroke went downwards and clove the horse's
spine.
Before him dead upon the field the man he hath o'erthrown.

Said Roland:
             "Thee hereafter for my brother will I own.
King Charlemagne aye loves us for such buffets with the
brand."
    Now was the war-shout of Mountjoy cried out on every
hand.

CIX. On the good charger Sorrel was Gerin the chevalier,
And Gerier his comrade on Swifter-than-the-Deer.
They slacked the rein together and spurred the horses well
And rode out to do battle with the Paynim Timosel.
On the shield smote one. The other his hauberk struck amain.
The two spears in his body were broken right in twain.
And of myself I know not, nor e'er did hear men say,
Which of the two good heroes was swiftest on that day.
And thither Count Espreveris the son of Borel drew.
Him, Engelier of Bordeaux in the battle overthrew.
And Turpin the Archbishop there slaughtered Siglorel,
The enchanter who already had descended into Hell.
There Jupiter had brought him by wicked glamourie.
    Said Turpin the Archbishop: "A strong villain was he."
And Roland spake in answer:
                          "The knave is vanquished here.
Beautiful are such gallant strokes, my brother Olivier."

CX. But the battle in the meanwhile in bitter guise outbroke.
The Frenchmen and the Paynims smote many a wondrous
stroke.
And some came on right fiercely; on their ward the others
stood.
What store of spears were shattered and drenchèd in the
blood!
How many gonfalons and flags were tattered in the fray.
How many gallant Frenchmen gave up their youth that day.
No more shall they see their mothers. Their wives they will
not see.
Nor the French beyond the passes that await them eagerly.
King Charlemagne he weeps and moans. Hath his woe any
worth?
They get thereby no succor. When Ganelon went forth
To sell in Saragossa his kindred for his gain,
He did most evil service to the men of Charlemagne.
But life and limb thereafter of the man went all to wreck.

In the court of Aix was he condemned. They hanged him by
the neck.
And thirty of his kinsmen perished with him thereby
That had not any deeming how they were doomed to die.

CXI. Marvellous waxed the battle with anguish heavy-
fraught.
And Olivier and Roland exceeding well they fought.
From the hand of the Archbishop a thousand strokes did fall,
Nor any whit were slothful the twelve peers one and all.
And all of the French army struck into the mellay.
By hundreds and by thousands the Paynims fell that day.
'Gainst death he had no warrant who fled not thence away
And, would he not or would he, his life was given o'er.
All of their fairest armor the Franks lost in the war.
Their fathers and their kinsmen they will never see again,
Nor him who waits beyond the gates, the Emperor Charle-
magne.
In France there was a tempest enough to make one quail.
Along the storm-cloud hasted with the thunder and the gale.
The rain and hail unmeasured beat fiercely from aloft;
And the thunder in its fury rattled many a time and oft.
And all the land was shaken by an earthquake verily
From Rheims unto Saint Michael-of-the-Peril-of-the-Sea,
And from the Port of Wissant unto Besançon the town
There was not any city whose bulwarks fell not down.
And at the height of noon-tide great darkness came on high;
There was no light nor clearness but for breaking of the sky.
All were in dread and many said:
                              "It is the day of doom.
The term of all our cycle and the end of time is come."
    The truth they understood not; no verity they spake.
It was sorrow for the paladin, and woe for Roland's sake.

CXII. The Franks have fought the battle with a great heart
and strong,
And the Paynim knights have fallen by thousands in the
throng.
Out of an hundred thousand are left but thousands two.
Said Turpin:
                "Our good cavaliers are gallant men to do.
Is no king under heaven has better in his ranks."
    This is the saying written in the deed-book of the Franks,

That the vassals of the Emperor are brave men in the fight.
Through the field they sought their comrades on the left and
on the right.
And the tears of grief and tenderness out of their eyes did
start
For love of their good kinsmen that were dear unto the heart.
   And with a great host Marsile the King before them stands.

CXIIa. I wot the great Count Roland is a good knight of his
hands.
And the twelve peers and Olivier great worship is their due.
The Paynims by their power in the fight they overthrew.
Of an hundred thousand homewards never a soldier came
Save for a single Paynim. Margaris was his name.
And though he fled, unto him shame or reproach was none.
His body bore him witness of the deeds that he had done.
Four lances had he in him. He turned back into Spain.
The matter of the battle to Marsile he made plain.

CXIIb. Alone hath the Count Margaris got safely from the
field.
His spear was broken in pieces, and piercèd was his shield,
And underneath the buckler but half a foot was left.
And as for his good helmet in pieces it was cleft.
And, moreover, of his hauberk all broken was the chain.
His good steel blade was ruddy with a vermilion stain.
And piercèd was his body with the strokes of four strong
spears.
Back he came from the battle where the buffets were so fierce.
God! what a baron had he been, had he been christened well.
Unto the Paynim Marsile those tidings did he tell.
Swiftly before the King he knelt and to him did he say:
   "To horse, my lord. The Franks of France are weary from
the fray
And from striking down our henchmen with the great strokes
of war.
They have lost the spears and bucklers that in the fight they
bore;
And half of all their army is slaughtered in the fight.
And they that yet are living are found in sorry plight.
The most are wounded and ruddy with the blood themselves
have shed;
And they have not any weapons against us to make head.
Lightly mayst thou avenge us. And now my master know

The army of King Charlemagne is ripe for overthrow."
  And to Roland and to Olivier the host of Frenchmen
prayed:
  "Let the twelve peers together come now unto our aid."
  And Turpin the Archbishop first of all his answer gave:
  "Ye men of God I pray you be of good heart and brave.
The crowns of God assuredly shall crown your heads this day,
And Paradise the Holy is your portion now for aye."
  Among the host of Frenchmen now was grief and sorrow
sad.
They wept in one another's arm for the friendship that they
had.
In charity they kissed. "Ye knights, to horse and ride along,"
Cried Roland, "Marsile cometh an hundred thousand
strong."

CXIII. And down amid a valley in haste King Marsile sped.
The army he had gathered along with him he led.
In twenty stricken columns their number had he told.
Blazing were all their helmets with precious stones and gold.
Pennants and spears and bucklers and broidered coats had
they,
And seven thousand war-horns were bellowing for the fray.
The bruit and the tumult through the land went far and near.
Said Roland:
                  "My good comrade and brother Olivier,
Count Ganelon, the traitor, hath sworn to work our death.
No longer may be hidden the breaking of his faith.
But certainly the Emperor shall well avenge the wrong.
And we will have a battle most terrible and strong.
There is no man that liveth that ever saw the like.
Therein with the blade Durendal the great strokes will I
strike.
Fall on, my good companion, with Haulteclair the brand.
Well, heretofore, the blades we bore in many and many a land.
And we have won together of battles such a throng.
Let them hereafter never sing of us an evil song."

CXIV. When the Franks looked on the heathen how fast
they came amain,
And how in every quarter they swarmed upon the plain,
Often then unto Roland and Olivier they prayed,
And the twelve peers, moreover, that they should stand their
aid.

And Turpin the Archbishop there made his meaning clear:
  "Ye gallant knights, I pray you that ye have no coward fear,
In God's name I beseech it. Turn not to flee away.
Let no brave man hereafter sing of you an evil lay.
Better it is in battle like a brave man to fall.
And this day it is certain we shall perish one and all.
After this day our fortune no longer is to live.
But for one thing unto you my warrant will I give.
For Holy Paradise is yours. With the Saints ye there shall dwell."
  When the Franks heard the Bishop's word it cheered them wondrous well.
There was not any Frenchman of them that stood about
But forthwith with a mighty voice Mountjoy began to shout.

CXIVa. Unto the worst of princes Marsile the King was peer.
He said unto the Paynims:
                    "Lordings, now hark and hear.
This Frank, the Marquis Roland, is a man of might and main.
Who will beat him in the battle must suffer grievous pain.
And Roland in two battles ye cannot overthrow.
But thrice, if it be your pleasure, against him will we go.
And ten of my strong columns against the French shall ride.
The other ten, however, shall tarry at my side.
The glory of King Charlemagne this day shall ruined be.
And France hurled into ruin, moreover, shall ye see."
  Then an embroidered banner he gave unto Grandoign
To lead his men against the Franks that battle they might join.
And therewithal was given to Grandoign the whole command.

CXIVb. To a low hill went Marsile and there he took his stand.
And Grandoign straight departed with all his company.
Down he rode through the valley as swiftly as might be.
His gonfalon was fastened with three fair nails of gold.
He shouted as he galloped:
                    "To horse, ye barons bold!"
And that it might be fairer yet a thousand trumpets blew.
"O Father God," the Frenchmen said,
                    "What deed is now to do?

Surely we saw Count Ganelon upon an evil day.
And by his wicked treason he has bartered us away.
What ho! the twelve companions! come now unto our aid!"
And first Archbishop Turpin gave answer there and said:
    "Good knights, to-day great honor unto you shall be given.
God will give you crowns and flowers amid the Saints of
Heaven.
But there is not any coward that shall enter into rest."
To him the Franks made answer:
                            "We will do thy whole behest.
We will not fear for death at all."
                            With the good golden spurs
They spurred away to battle against those dastard curs.
And they shouted all together: "Mountjoy for Charle-
magne!"

CXIVc. Marsile the king divided all of his host in twain.
Ten columns kept he with him and ten rode out to war.
A thousand trumpets thundered and a man might hear them
far.
    Said the Franks:
                    "God! what a slaughter shall we suffer in this
fray!
Ye twelve good peers, what deem you shall become of us
this day?"
    Thereto Archbishop Turpin spake in answer to this end:
"Good cavaliers, now greatly has God become your friend.
This day shall ye be crowned with crowns and lovely flowers
likewise;
This day ye shall have places in the peace of Paradise.
But never shall the cowards have any entry there."
    Said the Franks:
                    "We will not fail you in anything whate'er.
Never to God were it pleasing that we should be gainsaid.
With our full strength on the foemen this battle shall be made.
Few men we are, but hardy."
                            They spurred the knaves to slay
And Saracen and Frenchmen slashed into the mellay.

CXV. There was of Saragossa a Saracen at hand.
The half of all the city it was his fief and land.
'Twas Climborin who was not a good knight of his word.
'Twas he who with Count Ganelon had made a fast accord

That he should sell Count Roland and all his host of men.
Count Ganelon upon the mouth of friendship kissed he then,
And gave to him a carbuncle and therewithal his helm.
And he boasted there the Greater Land in shame to over-
whelm.
From Charlemagne would he take away the royal crown by
might.
He sate upon the charger that Barbamuche was hight:
And swifter than a swallow or a falcon was the steed.
He loosed the rein. He spurred him to the utmost of his speed.
Towards Engelier of Gascony he galloped o'er the field.
No whit might save the Frenchman his hauberk or his shield.
He thrust into the body the iron of the spear
So well that out behind him all of the point was clear.
With the swift lance upon the field he laid the dead man low.
And after cried:
              "These Frenchmen are good to overthrow.
Strike in! strike in! ye Saracens, and batter in their ranks."
   "God! what sorrow for the hero!" was the cry among the
Franks.

CXVI. And thereupon Count Roland to Olivier he said:
   "Engelier, lord companion, is already smitten dead.
We have not in the army a braver man than he."
   Said Olivier: "To venge him God grant it unto me."
   Forthwith he spurred the charger with the golden spurs
so good,
And he hove up the sword Haulteclair all ruddy with the
blood.
And there of his good courage he rode to smite him well.
His stroke hath made the Paynim reel; down from the steed
he fell.
And thence away his spirit the adversary bore;
Thereafter the Duke Alphaien he slaughtered in the war.
The brow of Escababi he clove it in his course,
And seven Arabs also he beat them from the horse.
Never again those seven men to war will take the path.
   Said Roland:
              "My companion is greatly up in wrath.
Beside me in the battle much honor now he hath.
We are dearer unto Charlemagne for such buffets as he
smites."
With a loud voice he shouted, "Strike into it, my knights!"

CXVII. Now came Valdabron the Paynim that for his chivalry
Marsile bred up. Four hundred ships were his upon the sea.
Was no sailor of his thieving but had sore cause to complain.
Jerusalem, the city, by treason had he ta'en.
The temple of King Solomon he plundered through and through.
The Patriarch, moreover, before the font he slew.
And Valdabron with Ganelon himself by oath had bound.
And a good sword he gave him and therewith a thousand pound.
There he sate in the saddle on Gradamont his horse.
Swifter than any falcon was that charger in his course.
He spurred right well. To fell him at Samson did he ride
That was a duke among the French, and a gallant man beside.
He shattered all the buckler, through the hauberk did he shear.
He thrust into the body the pennant of the spear.
With the swift lance from the saddle he smote the hero dead.
    "Knaves! ye shall die," with a great cry unto the French he said,
"This day an evil succor shall ye get from Charlemagne.
Paynims, strike in, and lightly this battle will we gain."
    Said the Franks: "God! for the baron how bitter is our woe."

CXVIII. When Roland saw Duke Samson slain in the overthrow,
Then he suffered such a sorrow as was never known to man.
He spurred the steed beneath him till its uttermost it ran;
And the sword worth more than the fine gold, even Durendal he bare.
Hard as he might he rode to smite against that Paynim there
A high stroke over his helmet of gold with the gems a-row.
He clove the head and the hauberk and the body with that blow,
And the good selle, that jewels and gold work did not lack,
Unto the back of the charger and deep into the back.
Whether ye praise or blame him, the twain there smote he dead.
    "A mighty stroke against us was that stroke," the Paynims said.
    "Ah! ever shall I hate you," shouted Roland through their throng,

"Upon your side is naught but pride and the bitterness of
wrong."

CXIX. An African of Africa into that battle came.
He was the son of Malcud; Malquidant was his name.
All of the gold fair beaten was the armour he had on.
Brighter than all the others was he flashing in the sun.
And he rode Lost-Leap, the charger with whom no beast
could race.
To smite the shield of Anseïs he galloped out apace.
The red and blue he pierced it, and the hauberk-plates he
broke.
He thrust both wood and iron through the body with the
stroke.
With the swift lance Lord Anseïs down on the field he bore.
The Count is dead. His season and his time of life are o'er.
    Said all the Franks, "Good baron, evil hap is on thy name."

CXX. Then spurring on his charger Archbishop Turpin came.
A priest the like of Turpin sang never Mass before.
That wrought with his own body such mighty deeds of war.
He said unto the Paynim:
                              "God's curse now fall on thee.
Thou hast slaughtered my good comrade and sore it irketh
me."
He spurred the steed and smote the wretch on the Toledo
shield
So that dead on the green herbage he struck him in the field.
    Now the son of Capuel the King of Cappadocia came
From the army of the heathen, and Grandoign was his name.
He sate upon the charger that Marmorie was hight,
A steed that was far fleeter than any bird in flight.
He spurred the charger with the spurs. He slacked the
bridle-rein,
He rode to fight with Gerin with all his might and main.
He rent the scarlet buckler with a great stroke in the fray;
Thereafter all his hauberk he tore and shore away.
He thrust into the body his azure battle-flag,
And dead he struck Count Gerin beside a mighty crag.
And his companion Gerier he likewise overthrew.
Guy of Saint Anton also, and Berenger he slew.
Then forth to fell Count Austore through the battle hastened
he,

Valentia on the Rhone that held as his own seignory.
He smote him dead. The Paynims were joyful one and all.
  Said the Franks to one another: "How fast our heroes fall!"

CXXII. A red sword had Count Roland. What lament the
Franks did make
He hearkened, and he sorrowed till his heart was like to break.
He said unto the Paynim:
                    "God's curse fall on thee here!
Thou hast slaughtered my companion. The thing shall cost
thee dear."
  He spurred the charger onwards that slackened not his
pace.
Whosoe'er shall lose the battle the twain are face to face.

CXXIII. Grandoign was stark and valiant and leal and keen
to fight.
He came on Roland in his way. He knew him at the sight,
Though never had he seen him, because of his proud glance,
By his look and his gentle body, and by his countenance.
He could not hide his terror and had fled, but naught availed,
For Roland with such fury the infidel assailed
That even through the nasal all of the helm was rent.
The stroke went down right through the crown. Unto the
teeth it went.
Through the body and the hauberk of the mail the buffet flew.
On the golden selle the pommel of silver it cut through,
And deep into the horse's back the good sword sank amain.
And horse and man upon the field fell cloven right in twain.
There rose among the Saracens a bitter wailing yell.
  Then said the Franks: "Our champion acquits him
wondrous well."

CXXIV. Marvellous was the battle and furious was the fight.
Fiercely the Franks struck into it in their anger and their
might.
They clove right through the Paynims, through back and side
and hand,
Through the garments of the living flesh with the keen
slashing brand.
And over the green grasses the blood went running clear.
  Quoth the Saracens:
                    "No longer can we bear the battle here.

Mahomet! on the Greater-Land black may thy curses fall,
For now before the nations her folk are best of all."
    There was no man among them King Marsile but implored:
    "Quickly to us that are in need! ride to our aid, our lord!"

CXXV. O wondrous is the battle, and terrible the tide.
The Franks with the brown-flashing spears hard into it
they ride.
The sorrow of the people there lightly might you view.
So many slain lay in their blood, deep smitten through and
through,
And outstretched or face downward on all sides were the dead.
Against the Franks the heathen no longer might make head.
And, would they not or would they, they turned their backs
in flight.
And all the Franks pursued them in their strength of living
might.

CXXVa. Roland wrought in the battle like a good knight and
strong,
And the Franks urged their horses most gallantly along.
At gallop and hand-gallop fled the Paynims as they could.
The Franks came on. Their bodies are stained with crimson
blood.
Twisted and bent and broken are the war-swords in the hand.
They have nought save the war-horns the foeman to with-
stand.
Then they thought upon the trumpets and the great horns
beside,
And he who had one by him was filled with strength and
pride.
With the horns the brows and bodies and the hands and feet
they clave.
Then said full many a Saracen:
                              "These Frenchmen are over brave.
There cometh now upon us the slaughter and the wrack."
They left the field behind them. On us they turned their back.
Great buffets with the war-horns the Frenchmen smote alway;
Even before King Marsile the line of dead men lay.

CXXVI. Marsile saw how in the slaughter his men were
overthrown.
His clarions and trumpets, he caused then to be blown.

Then out he rode to battle with his army of the ban.
Forth rode before a Saracen. Abysmus was the man.
There was not in that army a greater knave than he.
Vile crimes had he committed and filthy felony.
And of God, the Son of Mary, he trusted not the grace.
And blacker than the melted pitch was that Paynim in the face.
And better loved he treason and murder than to hold
At his pleasure all the treasure of the Galician gold.
Never had man beheld him to jest and laugh aloud.
He was a man of courage and furiousness uncowed.
Unto the foul King Marsile was he very dear therefore.
To rally men in battle the Dragon aye he bore.
And Turpin the Archbishop would never love that wight.
When he had looked upon him, he yearned the man to smite.
Under his breath the Bishop saith to himself quietly:
"A mighty heretic I deem this Saracen to be.
Better die than make no effort the villain here to slay.
Cowards to love and cowardice has never been my way."

CXXVII. Thereat Archbishop Turpin himself began the fray.
He sate upon a charger that from Grossail he had ta'en.
A king was he that Turpin in the Danish March had slain.
He was a coursing charger and swift to ride along.
His hoofs were seemly shapen. His legs were smooth and strong.
In the croup the steed was stalwart and narrow in the thigh;
His flanks were long and mighty; his back was very high.
White was his tail, and yellow from his neck the mane did fall,
And tawny was his frontlet, and his ears were fine and small.
There was no beast beneath the skies against him that could run,
And Turpin of his chivalry he spurred the courser on.
He slacked his hand on the bridle-rein and on the golden bit.
Until he smote Abysmus he waited not a whit.
To strike him on the wondrous shield against him did he bear,
Whereon was set a great array of precious stones and fair,
Amethyst, topaz, carbuncle, and crystal flaming clear.
They were given to Abysmus by Galáfer the Emir.
(Galáfer in Val-Metas from the fiend the jewels got)
But Turpin fell upon him and spared him not a jot.
After his stroke that buckler it was not worth a groat.

From side to side through the body Archbishop Turpin
smote.
He struck him down. Said all the Franks:
　　　　　　　　　　　　　"A gallant man is he.
Well enow with the Archbishop the Holy Cross will be."

CXXVIII. "Now by your leave, lord comrade," Roland
said to Olivier:
"This Turpin the Archbishop is a gallant cavalier—
Under the sky upon the earth better is none to fight.
Well hath he learned in battle with pike and spear to smite."
　And Olivier gave answer: "Let us go unto his aid."
And at the word the battle the Franks once more assayed.
Hard strokes, fierce thrusts the Christians bore, and agonies
most drear.
But though thereby they perish they will sell their lives right
dear.

CXXVIIIa. The Franks of France of weapons are in this
hour bereft.
No more than seven hundred of the naked swords are left.
They smite and cleave the helmets that are so fair of sheen.
God! What a store of bucklers through the midst are smitten
clean!
How many helms and hauberks broken in the field remain!
How many heads and hands and feet are smitten right in
twain!
Said the Paynims:
　　　　　　　　　"Lo, these Frenchmen they maim us every-
where.
The man that fleeth not away of life hath little care."
And right unto King Marsile the fliers held their way.
　"Lord King, now give us succor," unto him did they say.
When Marsile of his people the bitter cry had heard—
　"Now Lord Apollo aid me," even so he spake the word:
"Greater Land, by Mahomet mayst thou now be stripped
and strown.
Thine army hath mine army in the battle overthrown.
The Emperor white-bearded, the great King Charlemagne,
Calabria and Apulia and Rome itself hath ta'en,
Likewise Constantinople and stalwart Saxony.
Better it were to perish than before the French to flee.
Strike, Paynims! let no Frenchman deem himself safe at last.

If Roland die, then Charlemagne shall lose a stronghold fast,
And if he die not, all our lives are lost and overpast."

CXXVIIIb. Then stoutly with the lances fought those Pay-
nims unashamed.
They pierced through many bucklers with the great swords
that flamed.
They clove through many a helmet and many a hauberk
strong.
The steel and iron together sang such a fearful song
That up into the heavens the sparks of fire flew;
And blood and brains a-flowing there lightly might you view.
And because of this Count Roland had great dole and
heaviness,
As he looked on his good captains that died in their distress.
And thereon the Count remembered the land of France again,
And he thought upon his uncle the good King Charlemagne,
And a change came o'er his spirit that he could not stop or
stay.

CXXVIIIc. Count Roland hurled into the press, nor ceased
at all to slay.
Durendal the good warsword drawn in his hand he bore.
How many shields he shattered and pierced and clove in four!
How many hauberks did he burst and helms in pieces beat!
How many heads hath he cloven! How many hands and feet!
How many hundred Paynims on the field he killed in fight!
Nor was there any of them but thought himself a knight.

CXXVIIId. Olivier to the other side hath taken now the
track.
To smite against the Paynims he ran in the attack.
And the good sword, even Haulteclair, he held it up on high.
Save Durendal, a better was not beneath the sky,
Which Roland wielded. Strongly within the fight he stood.
Unto the arms was he spattered with the vermilion blood.
    "How gallant is he a vassal," said the lord Olivier,
"Woe unto us, our friendship this day shall fail us here.
It shall go in heavy sorrow. We are lost to Charlemagne.
In France shall be such sorrow as shall never be again.
There will be many a gallant man his prayer for us will make.
In holy churches orisons shall be offered for our sake
That our spirits into Paradise at last may go their course."

He loosed therewith the bridle-rein and onward spurred
the horse.
Through the press he came to Roland. To each other did
they call:
"Hither, comrade! I will fail thee not unless the first I fall."

CXXIX. Ah! to see Roland lift the sword, and likewise
Olivier!
But Turpin the Archbishop was fighting with a spear.
The number of the fallen lightly a man might tell—
In letters and in parchments is the matter written well.
The song saith more than thousands four of Saracens there
fell.
Through four attacks the Franks bore up, but heaviness and
pain
In the fifth fray overtook them. All the French knights were
slain.
Of the host no more than sixty whom God hath spared are by;
But dearly will they sell their lives before they come to die.

CXXX. Count Roland saw the slaughter of his men on every
side.
He turned him unto Olivier his comrade and he cried:
   "God bless thee, lord companion. Seest thou dead on
every hand
Our brave? Sore must we weep for France the sweet and
lovely land.
For lack of her good barons evil will be her cheer.
Oh, Charlemagne, our King and friend, wherefore wast thou
not here?
How may we send him tidings, my comrade Olivier?"
   Said Olivier:
                    "I know not how the thing may come to be.
But rather would I perish than that shame should come on
me."

CXXXI. Said Roland:
                         "On the war-horn now will I blow amain
And if within the passes the King shall hear it plain,
That again with the French army he will come, I will be
sworn."
   Olivier spake in answer:

"Thou wilt be held in scorn.
And a smirch and great dishonor on thy kinsmen would be
cast.
That shame would be upon them as long as life should last.
When I gave thereto my counsel, then naught of it wouldst
thou.
With my good will this matter thou shalt not compass now.
If thou blowest the horn, a deed thou dost the which no
brave man may.
And already those two arms of thine, scarlet with blood are
they."
   Thereto the Count gave answer, "Full fair strokes did I
smite."

CXXXII. And Roland said thereafter: "Most fearful is our
fight.
I will blow a blast that haply will be heard of Charlemagne."
   "When I urged it, friend," said Olivier, "To blow thou
wouldst not deign.
If but the King were with us we had not suffered so.
There lies no blame upon them that have yonder fallen low.
But by my beard I swear it: If I again set eye
On Aude my gentle sister, in her arms thou shalt not lie."

CXXXIII. Said Roland:
          "Wherefore at me in anger dost thou chide?"
"'Twas thine own doing, comrade," Count Olivier replied,
"For courage in good counsel with folly has no part.
And judgment aye is better than foolishness of heart.
And because of this thy vanity, lo, now the French are slain,
And our good deeds for ever are lost to Charlemagne.
And hadst thou but believed me, the King had come before,
We had compassed in this battle the ending of the war;
And either slain or taken King Marsile now would be.
Ah, Roland, in thy hardihood an evil thing we see.
Thy service unto Charlemagne thou never more shalt pay.
Never shall be his like again until the Judgment Day.
Thou wilt perish. At the land of France shall men shoot out
the lip.
And to-day, moreover, endeth our good companionship.
In woe we shall be parted or e'er come Vesper-tide."

CXXXIV. Swiftly Turpin galloped to them when he had
heard them chide.
Spurring with golden spurs his steed; and the twain did he
chastise:
   "O, thou my good Lord Roland, and Lord Olivier likewise,
Now by my God I pray you your wrath to put away,
For in no wise the war-horn may stand our stead to-day.
But ne'ertheless is it better thereon to blow the blast.
Hither will come King Charlemagne and avenge us at the
last.
Never again the Spaniards light-hearted hence shall speed.
Here will our own dear Frenchmen dismount them from the
steed.
Here will they find us stark and dead smitten with many a
wound;
On biers upon the sumpter-beasts will they raise us from the
ground.
They will mourn for us in pity and in sorrow, one and all,
And bury us together within the convent-wall.
Nor wolf nor hound shall devour us, nor wild boar on us feed."
   And Roland spake in answer: "Thou speakest well
indeed."

CXXXV. The mighty horn Count Roland hath put his lips
unto.
He held it well between them, and with all his strength he
blew.
And high are all the summits, and O the way is long,
But a full fifteen good leagues away they heard it echo strong.
And Charlemagne hath heard it, and his every knave and
knight.
   Said Charlemagne: "Our henchmen have fallen on some
fight."
   But Ganelon unto him hath spoken in reply,
"Had any other said it thou wouldst take it for a lie."

CXXXVI. Even so the Marquis Roland in agony and pain
And bitterness of sorrow blew on the horn amain.
Out of his mouth in a great spurt the clear blood gushing went.
Of his fair brow by the effort was the temple burst and rent.
Of the war-horn that he blew on the thunder was so great
That Charlemagne hath heard it within the mountain-gate.
Neimes the Duke hath hearkened it, and the Franks heard
it plain.

"I hear the horn of Roland," said the Emperor Charle-
magne.
"And never would he blow it unless a fight were on."
"There is no battle toward," then answered Ganelon,
"But now thy hair is hoary and thy locks white as snow.
Thou seemest like unto a babe what time thou speakest so.
Certes! enough thou knowest how great is Roland's pride.
Strange is it God hath suffered him so long while to abide.
Without thine order Nobilis the city did he win.
There sallied out against him the Saracens therein.
Against Roland the good vassal they lifted up the hand.
He delivered them to slaughter with Durendal the brand.
And the blood from the green meadows he washed with
water there.
He did the thing that it might seem more fitting and more fair.
For a lone hare the war-horn all the day long doth he wind.
He rideth jesting on ahead with all his peers behind.
Under sky is none that dareth meet Roland in the fray.
My Lord the King ride onward. For wherefore should we
stay?
Ye may behold the Greater Land how far it is ahead."

CXXXVII. Now the lips of the Count Roland with spurting
blood were red,
He blew upon the war-horn in dolor and in pain.
And all the Frenchmen hearkened and the Emperor
Charlemagne.
And the King spake:
                    "Yon war-horn it hath a mighty breath.
A hero bloweth in anguish." Neimes in answer saith:
    "I deem there is battle. Roland is mastered by some
sleight.
This knave would trick thee. Cry thy cry and arm thee for the
fight,
If to the gallant army succor may yet avail.
Here hast thou hearkened overlong how Roland tells the
tale."

CXXXVIII. The Emperor his war-horns forthwith he let
them peal.
From the steeds the Franks dismounted and girded on the
steel.
The hauberks and the helmets and the great swords of gold,
And splendid shields and lances heavy and strong they hold,

With the vermilion gonfalons, and the azure and the white.
There mounted on the chargers of the army every knight.
Hot-spurred they sped through the defile. To his fellow each
man said:
   "If we may look on Roland or ever he is dead,
Then may we with him lightly deal mighty strokes and
strong."
   What profit in their courage? They have tarried overlong.

CXXXIX. At length the darkness lightened. The day was
coming on,
And all the armor of the host was flashing in the sun.
The hauberks and the helmets shone with a mighty glare,
And likewise the good bucklers with flowers painted fair,
And gleaming were the lances and the gonfalons of gold.
The Emperor in anger his way along did hold.
And the Franks were very angry, and of very evil cheer.
Was none but in his sorrow shed many a bitter tear.
For the safety of Count Roland they were all in mighty fear.
And Charlemagne the Emperor let Ganelon be ta'en.
To the cooks within his kitchen he delivered him amain.
Bégon the master of the cooks he charged most heavily
   "This fellow like a traitor do thou watch and ward for me
That betrayed my house."
                       And Bégon took the Count in custody.
Of the best and worst an hundred of the kitchen-fellowship
Put he o'er him, and they pulled the beard on the Count's
chin and lip.
And every one to Ganelon with the fist four buffets gave,
And thereafter beat him nobly with the twig and with the
stave.
And a mighty chain about his neck they forced the man to
wear.
They chained him in no otherwise than as men chain a bear.
And high upon a sumpter-beast they set him in disdain.
Thus they kept him till they gave him to the hands of
Charlemagne.

CXL. Darkling are all the summits and very great and high,
And deep are all the valleys and the streams run swift thereby.
In van and rear the war-horns sounded up and down the
track;
To the great horn of Roland they gave their answer back.

And aye they prayed unto their God that Roland he would
shield,
Till they were come unto him upon the battle-field.
They will strike with him verily. What worth that they are
strong?
Naught worth! They may not come in time. They have
tarried overlong.

CXLI. And Charlemagne the Emperor in mighty anger sped.
Down on his battle-hauberk his great white beard it spread.
In fiery haste along with him the Frankish barons spurred.
There was no man among them but spoke a bitter word,
For that with the Captain Roland they were not standing
then,
What time he joined the battle with the Spanish Saracen.
Of his host, if he be wounded, no soul alive will be.
Ah, what a gallant sixty yet keep him company!
There is no king or captain hath better men than he.

CXLII. Over the heaths and mountains looked Roland
every way,
And he saw dead upon the field how thick the Frenchmen lay.
And like unto a courteous knight sore he bewailed their case:
    "Ah now my fair lord barons! God grant you His sweet
grace.
And permit unto your spirits His Paradise to share;
And cause you to lie down among the holy flowers there.
A better sort of vassal I never yet did see.
For a great time good service have ye ever yielded me.
For the Emperor many nations ye conquered in your power;
But he undertook your governance in a very evil hour.
O land of France, my country that is so sweet and bright,
To-day hast thou lost forever full many a gallant knight.
Lords of the Franks I saw you, how for my sake ye fell;
And I could not defend you nor send you succor well.
May God who never lieth henceforth have you in His hand.
But Olivier my comrade now with thee will I stand.
I will perish of this sorrow, if here I be not slain.
Ho! now my lord companions, let us into it again!"

CXLIII. And forthwith the Count Roland hied him down
into the field.
Like to a furious hero the warsword did he wield.

And Falbron of the Peak that tide through the midst he clove
in two;
And four and twenty others of the best he overthrew.
Never was man in vengeance had more fearful a delight.
Even as the stag that runneth before the hounds in flight,
Even so before Count Roland the Paynim army fled.
    "Thou dost thy duty fairly," Archbishop Turpin said.
"It is this sort of courage every knight should have indeed.
That beareth any armor and sitteth on a steed.
He ought in the high battles both stout and stark to be.
Otherwise are four farthings of better worth than he.
A monk in a monastery he should hide himself away,
And pray for our deliverance from our ill deeds each day."
    Roland answered:
                "Smite and spare not." They began again the war;
But in the fray the Christians a mighty loss they bore.

CXLIV. When that there was no quarter was known to
every wight,
There was no man but furiously went down into the fight.
And therefore all the Frenchmen like lions wood were they.
Lo! now is come King Marsile like a hero of the fray.
On the steed Gaignon spurring hard, he came, and hath
o'erthrown
Bevon that was the hero of Dijon and of Beaune.
He burst right through the hauberk; the shield he broke in
twain.
Without ado the hero he struck him down amain;
And Ivoris, moreover, and Ivo hath he slain,
And Gerard of Roussillon therewith. Roland not far was he.
    He said unto the Paynim:
                "The Lord God's curse on thee!
With little right or reason my comrades didst thou slay.
Thou shalt feel my heaviness of hand, e'er we depart this day;
And thou shalt know, moreover, the name of this my brand."
    Like a knight he went to smite him and cut off his right
hand.
And then he has smitten off the head of Jorfaleu the Fair.
Of the Saracen King Marsile he was the son and heir.
The Paynims cried:
                "Mahomet aid! Our gods on Charlemagne
Wreak vengeance for the villains he marshalled into Spain.
Rather than yield the battle-field unto us, will they die."

Said one unto the other: "Then forthwith let us fly."
At the word an hundred thousand, to the rear they took the
track.
Never more will they turn again, whoever calls them back.

CXLIVa. King Marsile his right hand hath lost, and Jorfaleu
lies dead.
To earth he cast the shield. The steed sharply he spurred,
and fled.
He loosed the rein away to Spain. An hundred thousand
strong
Was the number of the fliers that went with him along.
There was not one among them but he was wounded sore.
Said each to each: "The nephew of King Charles hath won
the war."

CXLV. What profits it, if Marsile his flight away hath ta'en?
Yet doth his eme the Algalif upon the field remain.
He ruled in Cartagéna, Alferne and Garmalie,
And Ethiopia accursed, and in his seignory
Was the Negro race. Great noses and mighty ears have they.
And more than fifty thousand were gathered for the fray.
And they came riding thither in mighty wrath and proud.
The war-cry of the Paynims they lifted up aloud.
    Cried Roland:
                    "Unto martyrdom now are we given o'er
In my heart I understand it that we shall live no more.
But let him be accursèd his life that sells not dear
Now with the shining war-sword smite every cavalier.
Now with a mighty challenge your life and death defend,
That ne'er on the sweet realm of France through you shall
shame descend.
When to the field hereafter cometh King Charlemagne,
And seeth of the Paynims what a multitude are slain,
And that for every one of us fifteen of them are dead,
He will not cease from pouring his blessings on our head."

CXLVI. But when that the Count Roland had seen the
accursèd race,
Whereof each man of them than ink was blacker of his face,
(Save for the teeth was every man among them even so)
Then spake the Count:
                    "Now verily I understand and know

That every man among us shall perish on this day.
Strike, Franks! Anew in your behalf will I take up the fray."
　　Quoth Olivier: "Misfortune on the faint-hearted light."
And at the word the Frenchmen hurled down into the fight.

CXLVII. When the Paynims saw the Frenchmen that their
number was so small,
In comfort and in joyance they cheered them one and all.
　　"God is not with the Emperor," one to the other said.
There was the Algalif, that sate upon a charger red.
With the golden spurs he spurred him, and running from
the rear
Full in the back a dreadful stroke he smote on Olivier.
And the white hauberk on him from his body there he clove;
Through his breast forth of the breast-bone the bitter lance
he drove.
Thereto he said unto him:
　　　　　　　　　　　"Thou hast ta'en thy stroke of fate.
In an evil hour King Charlemagne hath left thee in the gate.
He hath wrought us wrong exceeding, but thereof he shall
not boast,
For well enough on thee alone have I avenged our host."

CXLVIII. And Olivier knew forthwith that his death wound
he bore.
Before he should avenge himself he would not tarry more.
On high he lifted Haulteclair whereof the steel flashed brown.
On the Algalif's bright golden helm he brought the great
strokes down.
At a blow the gems and flowers unto the ground he sped;
And straight into two pieces he clove the Paynim's head.
He brandished o'er the Algalif, and slew him at the stroke.
　　"My curse upon thee, Paynim." Thus he thereafter spoke:
"I say not that no loss at all is come on Charlemagne;
But unto any woman thou wilt not go again
To boast thyself in any way in the country of thy birth
How thou hast ta'en from Charlemagne a single farthing's
worth,
Nor the havoc that on others and upon me thou hast made."
　　After he called to Roland that he might bring him aid.

CXLIX. That his sore wound was mortal, Olivier knew
inwardly;

But he deemed that it was not enough himself avenged to be.
Once more to smite like a good knight into the press he
wheeled.
There he cut through the lances and many a buckled shield,
And fist and foot and shoulder, and likewise many a side.
Who that champion a-hewing at the Saracens descried,
And hurling down their bodies o'er each other in a pile,
The deeds of a good vassal might keep in mind the while.
And still not yet could he forget Charlemagne's battle-cry.
"Mountjoy!" he kept a-shouting in a clear voice and high,
And to Roland his good comrade with a loud voice did he say:
"Draw nigh, fair friend. In sorrow we twain must part this
day."

CL. Roland looked upon Olivier, that was livid and pale and
wan.
The clear blood from his body, forth in a spurt it ran.
Down to the ground went dropping the great clots of the gore.
    "God!" said Count Roland, "What to do I know not any
more.
Lord comrade, mighty evil has wrought thy chivalry.
Of his body none for courage shall ever equal thee.
Sweet land of France, how barren art thou this day, and
waste
Of all thy gallant heroes, and confounded and disgraced.
The Emperor in this slaughter will have great loss indeed."
    The word he scarce had spoken when he fainted on the
steed.

CLI. Lo! now the Marquis Roland on his charger in a swound,
And likewise the Lord Olivier that hath a mortal wound.
And his eyes are growing troubled (his blood has run so free).
The far and near no longer could the knight clearly see,
Nor had he longer power to know any mortal man.
And when on the Count Roland his comrade dear he ran,
On the helmet gemmed and golden he smote him from above,
And the whole of the good helmet from the nasal down he
clove,
But the head it did not injure. Roland looked up at the stroke
And unto his companion in a gentle voice he spoke:
    "Of thy free-will, my brother, thus dost thou smite me
here?

Wottest thou that I am Roland who holdeth thee so dear?
Neither in any fashion yet hast thou challenged me."
    Said Olivier:
                "I hear thee speak. I got no sight of thee.
 God keep thee! If I smote thee thy pardon will I cry."
    And Roland spoke in answer:
                        "No hurt I have thereby.
Here I give thee my pardon, and before our God on high."
And at the word each champion bowed his head before his
peer.
And thus it was they parted that each other held so dear.

CLII. Olivier felt come o'er him death and its agony.
His eyes were whirling in his head. He could not hear or see.
Down from the steed he got him, and on the ground did lie.
Of the ill deeds of his doing he confessed him loud and high.
That he might enter Paradise to God he made his prayer.
He gave his benediction to Charles and France the fair,
And to his comrade Roland over all the sons of men.
But his heart failed within him and his head he lowered then.
And therewith all his body along the ground it spread.
It was no skill to tarry. Count Olivier was dead.
Roland beheld and wept aloud, lamenting in his woe.
Never ye saw upon the earth a man that sorrowed so.

CLIII. But when looked the Count Roland on his dead
friend in the place,
And saw him how he lay there that eastward turned his face,
He 'gan softly to bewail him:
                      "Ill for thee, good cavalier,
Was thy might. We were together for many a day and year.
Never ill service gavest thou me, nor I to thee did give.
Now thou art dead, great evil I deem it that I live."
    In the sorrow that he suffered a swound upon him came,
Where he sate upon the charger that Valiant had to name.
But in the stirrups of fine gold firmly were set his feet.
He could not whereso'er he went slip downwards from the
seat.

CLIV. Scarce had he come unto himself and wakened from his
swound,
When the greatness of the slaughter was clear to him around.

The Franks were dead. The army was lost and overthrown,
Save for Archbishop Turpin and Walter-a-Hume alone,
From the mount that came, where nobly he had fought the
men of Spain.
The Saracen had won the day and all his men were slain.
He fled into the valley, whether or no it be gainsaid,
And he shouted unto Roland that he should bear him aid;
    "O gentle Count and valiant man, I prithee where art
thou?
Afraid would I be never, if I were with thee now.
I am Walter that o'er Maëlgut got once the overthrow,
The nephew of Lord Droün with the beard as white as snow.
I was wont to be thy comrade, for my spirit did not quail.
Now lance and shield are shattered, and broken is my mail.
I am thrust through the body with lances overwell;
But myself unto the Saracens right dearly did I sell "
    When that he heard Lord Walter's word, the man Count
Roland knew,
And spurring up the charger unto the knight he drew.

CLIVa. "Lord Walter," said Count Roland, "I deem thou
hast been in fight.
Thou hast fought very bravely as becomes a gallant knight.
A thousand valiant cavaliers to the battle didst thou lead.
Give them to me, for of them I have most bitter need."
    And Walter answered:
                        "Living shalt thou never see them more.
I have left them dead behind me on that dolorous field of war.
There found we at encounter a great army Saracen,
Persians and Turks and Arabs and the Armenian men,
Algolans and men of Beda. Fiercely we fought that host.
No Paynim to another thereof shall make his boast;
For of them sixty thousand dead on the field remain.
But there in that same battle all of our Franks were slain.
For ourselves with the swords of iron we wrought a ven-
geance great.
Of the hauberk here upon me broken is every plate.
And I have wounds a-plenty my flank and side about.
From all parts of my body the clear blood spurteth out.
And everywhere I weaken and I deem that I shall die.
And I seek thee for deliverance, for thy sworn man am I.
And prithee do not blame me that from the fight I fled."

"Nay! never will I do it," in answer Roland said,
"Thou hast suffered much, companion, and a great agony,
But so long as life endureth, lend thou thine aid to me."

CLV. Roland was filled with anger and likewise bitter wrath.
Again into the battle he began to hew his path.
There hath he given to slaughter twenty of the men of Spain,
And six were killed by Walter, and five hath Turpin slain.
  "These be ill knaves," said the Paynims, "Hence alive let
them not flee.
Who comes not up against them, accursèd let him be,
And a vile knave who lets them scape." They raised the hue
and cry.
And now from every quarter to the onslaught they drew nigh.

CLVI. Proud is the Marquis Roland, and hardy is his heart.
Walter-a-Hume beside him like a good knight played his part;
And Turpin the Archbishop is a good man and tried;
In no way any of the three would leave his fellow's side.
They thrust into the heathen press in courage and in might.
A thousand of the Paynims from their horses did alight.
But a full forty thousand upon their steeds were there,
In my belief that nearer to approach them did not dare.
At the Franks the spears and lances were they hurling and
the like,
The throwing-dart and javelin, the arrow and the pike.
And there at the first volley Walter-a-Hume they slew.
Turpin of Rheims his buckler they pierced it through and
through.
They have broken through his helmet and wounded sore
his head,
And as for his good hauberk they rended it and shred.
And right into his body four spears were driven grim.
And the Paynims slew, moreover, the charger under him.
It was an evil hour when the Bishop bit the dust.

CLVII. When he knew that he was stricken, and four spears
were through him thrust
Swiftly he leaped unto his feet, and to Roland turned his
head.
And forthwith ran unto him. But a single word he said:
"Not yet am I beaten. Living no true man e'er is ta'en."
Almace, the great brown blade of steel, he plucked it out
amain.

A thousand strokes in the great press he dealt there to and
fro.
Thereafter said King Charlemagne that he let not any go.
A full four hundred corpses about him there were found.
None was there but was cloven through or bore a deadly
wound.
And from some the heads were smitten (in the Deed Book is
it writ,
And they that were upon the field likewise attested it).
Saint Giles the knight, in whose behoof God wrought His
wonders great,
In Laon Monastery the matter did relate.
And he who speaketh other, thereof he knoweth naught.

CLVIII. Meanwhile the Marquis Roland in fearful guise he
fought.
But his body was all sweating and burning as with fire.
His head was like to break in twain with agony most dire,
And broken were his temples for the blowing of the blast,
But he yearned to know the tidings whether Charles would
come at last.
He drew the great horn to him; thereon he feebly blew.
The Emperor halted in the pass. The trumpet call he knew.
    "My lords," said he, "Most certainly we are in evil way.
Count Roland, my good nephew, is lost to us this day.
I know him by his blowing that his life is nearly gone.
Whoso'er would reach the battle let him prick his charger on.
Blow each horn in the army."
                            There blew sixty thousand strong.
Bellowing from vale to mountain echoed the sound along.
The Paynims heard. They jested not concerning that refrain.
Said one unto the other: "At hand is Charlemagne."

CLIX. Said the Paynims:
                    "Once more hither the Emperor draws near.
And of the Frankish army the war-horns ye may hear.
If Charlemagne returneth we shall be smitten sore;
And if Count Roland liveth he will wage anew the war;
And Spain is taken from us that was our own good realm."
    Forthwith with a full four hundred were gathered under helm.
The fiercest soldiers on the field in fury made attack
Upon the Marquis Roland that labor did not lack.

CLX. But when the Marquis Roland beheld them how they
came,
Then was he fierce and mighty and ready for the game.
Nor will he yield him to them while life within him stirs.
He leaped on Valiant and pricked him with the good golden
spurs.
And rushed to slaughter 'mid the press, and with him Turpin
sped.
   "Flee hence away, good comrades," each to each the
Paynims said.
"Of the French host the war-horns ye may hear them far and
wide.
Hither again doth Charlemagne the mighty Emperor ride."

CLXI. Count Roland loved no craven nor proud nor haughty
wight,
Nor ever any cavalier that was not a faithful knight.
He called to Bishop Turpin:
                    "Lo! on thy feet art thou,
And I a-horse; of charity I will halt beside thee now.
Let us abide together the evil and the good.
I will not quit thee for any that is made of flesh and blood.
This day in this same battle well shall the Paynims know.
The name of the sword Almace and Durendal also."
   "'Tis a knave his best who strikes not," Turpin said to him
again.
"At his return great toll for us shall take King Charlemagne."

CLXII. Said the Paynims:
                 "Very evil was our fortune to be born.
And the day was very dreadful that broke for us this morn.
We had sore loss of many a lord and many a gallant peer.
With his great host Charles the Captain again returneth here.
We hearken the clear war-horn of the Frenchmen blowing
high.
Loud is the thunder of Mountjoy that is their battle-cry.
As for the Marquis Roland so terrible is he,
That not in fight by mortal man e'er vanquished will he be.
Give him now room; cast at him, standing from him apart."
   At him was many a javelin flung, and many a throwing
dart,
And many a feathered arrow and many a lance and spear.

They pierced and rent his buckler, and made havoc of his
gear.
They hurt not Roland's body, but the steed Valiant through
They smote in thirty places, and 'neath the Count they slew.
They let him bide and swiftly they turned away in flight.
Roland was left there standing upon the field of fight.

CLXIII. In sore haste fled the Paynims and in anger and in
wrath.
Hard back into the land of Spain, now have they turned
their path.
In no wise did Count Roland follow upon their course.
He had lost within the battle Valiant his gallant horse;
And, would he not or would he, in the place afoot he stayed.
Unto Archbishop Turpin he went to bear him aid.
And he unlaced, moreover, the golden helmet bright.
And he loosened the white hauberk, so fair that was and light.
He divided the good tunic, and many a wound he dressed
With pieces of the garment and bound them with the rest.
Then to his heart the Bishop he held in an embrace,
And down he softly laid him in a green grassy place
And gently prayed:
                    "Ah, goodly man, give me thy leave to go!
Our comrades whom we held so dear have met their over-
throw.
We must not leave them. I will seek and find them where
they be,
And bring them straightway hither, and rank them here by
thee."
    Said Turpin the Archbishop:
                    "Go and return apace.
Thou and I have won the battle through God's exceeding
grace."

CLXIV. Then Roland turned from Turpin. Alone through
the field he hied.
He searched along the valley; he searched the mountain-side.
On Ivoris and Ivo and Gerier he fell,
And Gerin his good comrade, and Berenger as well.
On Othon and on Samson and Anseïs came he,
And likewise upon Engelier the man of Gascony.
And with them Gerard the old man of Roussillon he found.

And one by one the barons he lifted from the ground,
And forth unto the Bishop each one of them he bore.
In a long rank he ranged them the Bishop's knees before,
That could not keep from weeping. But he lifted up his hand
And blessed them and said:
                              "Lord barons, in evil stead ye stand.
By the great God now may your souls be raisèd up and ta'en,
And amid the holy flowers be suffered to remain.
In very bitter anguish my death comes over me,
And nevermore King Charlemagne the splendid will I see."

CLXV. Count Roland o'er the battle field went seeking far
and near,
And at the last discovered his comrade Olivier.
And straitly to his bosom he clasped the dead man there.
And as he might with the body to the Bishop did he fare.
On a shield beside his fellows he laid the dead to rest.
And there Archbishop Turpin has absolved them all and blest.
And now his pain and pity waxed great without an end.
"Oh Olivier," said Roland, "my fair and lovely friend,
Thou wert son to the Duke of Genoa the gallant lord Rainier.
To batter through the buckler, to shatter the strong spear,
To overthrow the arrogant and to dismay their pride,
And gallant men and heroes to counsel and to guide,
And villains aye to conquer and to fill them with affright,
Ne'er in the girth of all the earth was there a better knight."

CLXVI. But when Count Roland cast his eye on the corpse
of each dead peer,
And on Olivier, moreover, whom he had held so dear,
Then straightway he began to weep, he felt such tenderness;
And the color of his visage was changed in his distress.
He had so great a sorrow that its like might not be found.
And, would he not or would he, he fainted on the ground.
    Said Turpin unto Roland: "Thou art come on an evil
day."

CLXVII. When well had the Archbishop seen how Roland
swooned away,
Then sorrowed he so bitterly that so greatly none might
mourn.
He reached his hand to Roland and got hold upon the horn.
There was in Roncevaux hard by a running water spring.

He would go there that water to Roland he might bring.
He put great force upon him. And on his feet he got.
With little steps and feeble he went tottering towards the
spot.
He was so weak he might not walk. He had lost such store
of blood
That he had no strength or courage. Ere he had gone a rood
His heart gave way within him. Forward he fell again;
And his own death came on him in a great burst of pain.

CLXVIII. Meanwhile the Marquis Roland out of his swound
arose.
Upon his feet he got him, but grievous were his woes.
Above him and below him his eyes wandered away.
Beyond his friends on the green grass he saw where Turpin
lay,
That good baron the Archbishop, God's embassador. On high
Looked Turpin and confessed him with his eyes unto the sky.
He prayed God to enter Heaven. Charlemagne's knight was
dead.
By the great fights he fought in, by the good words that he
said.
Ever against the Paynims had he kept up the war.
His Holy Benediction God give to him therefor.

CLIX. Roland looked on the Archbishop where he lay
upon the earth,
And saw out of his body the bowels gushing forth.
He saw on the rent forehead the brains come bubbling
through,
And flowing down upon his breast between his shoulders two.
The two white hands together he crossed that were so fair.
After the custom of the land he mourned for Turpin there:
    "Ah! man of fair conditions and lineage great and high,
This day to God I give thee, the ruler of the sky,
Never man did His service than thou more willingly.
None was since the apostles so great in prophecy;
Nor to keep the law of Christians, nor heathen to convert.
May now thy spirit therefore suffer no kind of hurt.
Of Paradise may now the gates for thee be open thrown."

CLXX. Count Roland knew in spirit that his own death came
on.

For his own brains in that hour were bursting from his ears.
That God might take them to Him, he prayed for all the
peers.
Then to the Angel Gabriel for his own sake he prayed.
He seized the horn that no reproach against him might be
made,
And Durendal the war-sword in the other hath he ta'en.
Farther than crossbow shoots the bolt into the land of Spain
To a meadow and a hillock in the meadow mounted he.
There were four great steps of marble under a noble tree.
And down on the green herbage backward he fell thereby.
There hath he swooned and fainted, for his death drew very
nigh.

CLXXI. Oh lofty were the mountains and tall the trees
each one.
There were four great steps fashioned of glistening marble-
stone.
But there spied on him a Saracen that death nearby had
feigned,
Lying with the dead. His body and his face with blood were
stained.
Forthwith he got upon his feet. He hastened and he ran.
He was beautiful and mighty and a very hardy man.
And anger rose within him for his heart was full of pride.
He seized on Roland's body and his weapons, and he cried:
    "Vanquished is Charles's nephew. His sword now will I
take
To Araby."
                As he touched it, somewhat the Count did wake.

CLXXII. Roland felt how the Paynim strove then to lift
the sword.
He oped his eyes, and to him said but a single word:
    "Thou art after my deeming no soldier of our host."
    He lifted up the war-horn that he had not lightly lost.
Right on the jewelled helmet he smote him such a stroke
That he shattered all the iron, and brow and skull he broke.
Both of the eyes together were beaten from his head.
Right at the feet of Roland was the Paynim stricken dead.
    "To lay thine hand upon me," said he, "thou Paynim
knave,
With right or else with unright, what made thee now so
brave?

For a fool all men hereafter shall hold thee now in scorn.
Broken into many pieces is the great bell of mine horn
The jewels and the gold-work are wrenched away and torn."

CLXXIII. Well knew the good Count Roland that his death
was hard at hand.
His strength he strove to gather, and on his feet did stand.
The color from his visage forth was driven and dispelled,
And in his hand the naked brand, even Durendal, he held.
Before him was a great brown stone amidmost of his path.
Ten strokes he smote upon it in agony and wrath.
Grided the steel but broke not. No notch was on the blade.
"Ah," said the Count, "St. Mary come now unto my aid.
Ah, Durendal! good war-sword, evil is thy destiny.
The day whereon I lose myself I cannot care for thee.
Many battles I won with thee, many lands did overthrow,
Where now doth reign King Charlemagne with the beard
as white as snow.
Mayst thou ne'er be his possession, for another that will flee.
For it was a good vassal that a long time carried thee.
In the land of France another his like there will not be."

CLXXIV. Roland upon the sardine stone a mighty stroke
let fall.
Grided the steel but broke not, nor was it notched at all.
And when he had beheld it that the sword he could not break
Unto himself a bitter moan he then began to make:
   "O Durendal, how art thou so beautiful and white!
Flashing and flaming in the sun thou scatterest the light.
What time Charlemagne had halted in the Vale of
Maurienne
God out of Heaven an angel sent down unto him then,
And bade him to a noble count a gift to make of thee.
And the gentle King and mighty girded thee there on me.
For him I won all Brittany, Anjou, Poitou, and Maine,
And the free land of Normandy, Provence and Aquitain.
The Roman March and Lombardy I conquered to his hand,
I won beside Bavaria and all the Flemish land.
Bulgaria and Poland by me were overthrown,
Also Constantinople that Charles for king did own.
All Saxony, moreover, his whole behest hath done.
And Ireland, Wales and Scotland for Charlemagne I won,
And the English island likewise, that he took of his own right.
A many lands and nations I conquered in the fight,

That now are the possession of white-bearded Charlemagne.
Wherefore I suffer for this sword great pity and great pain.
I had rather die than a Paynim should win it by ill chance.
Fair God! let such dishonor fall never upon France."

CLXXV. Again the sword of Roland down on the dark stone
fell.
He smote more oft and harder than I know how to tell.
Grided the sword upon the stone, but shattered not nor broke.
Back again into heaven it rebounded from the stroke.
And when the Count beheld it that unbroken was the blade,
Then very softly to himself his sore complaint he made:
    "Ah, Durendal! how holy and virtuous art thou!
Within thy golden pommel relics there are enow.
The tooth of good Saint Peter, and Saint Basil's blood are
there,
And of my Lord Saint Denis a lock of sacred hair,
And of the Virgin's vesture a little part and share.
A possession of the Paynims thou oughtest not to be.
In battle should a Christian forever carry thee.
Ah, may no man that bears thee ever have a coward's name,
For many were the nations that with thee I overcame,
Wherein doth reign King Charlemagne with the great beard
like a flower.
Strong thereby is the Emperor and full of utter power."

CLXXVI. When Roland knew his death hour how hard on
him it pressed,
And that death was slowly creeping from his brow unto his
breast,
Under a pine he hastened, and down his body laid
On the green grass. Beneath him he placed his horn and
blade.
And unto the great land of Spain he turned his head away.
He did the thing for sore he yearned that Charlemagne
might say
And all his host: "A conqueror the gallant Count has died."
And he made confession duly and for forgiveness cried,
And his glove to God he offered for the ill deeds he had done.

CLXXVII. When well had Roland seen it that his time of
life was gone,
There abode he on the mountain-peak that turneth unto
Spain;

There with one hand his bosom he smote on it amain:
    "Forgive Thou mine iniquities of Thy mercy, one and all,
All of my evil doings, the great ones and the small
That I have done upon the earth since the day that I was
born
Unto this day, wherein I was much smitten and forlorn."
    His right glove to God in Heaven he reached it up on high,
And God His angels to him flew down out of the sky.

CLXXVIII. Count Roland neath a pine-tree down on the
ground has lain,
And far away he turned his glance unto the land of Spain.
And many things together were remembered of the knight:
What a great store of nations he had conquered in the fight.
He thought on the sweet land of France and of his kindred
dear,
And on Charlemagne his master that erewhile did him rear.
And he could not keep from sobbing, and he wept in his dis-
tress.
Yet he let not his spirit perish in forgetfulness.
For he prayed to God for mercy, and his guilt aloud he cried
Clearly to God:
                    "Ah very God that never yet hath lied,
Ah, God! who brought Saint Lazarus in glory from the grave,
Who succor 'gainst the lion to the Prophet Daniel gave,
Guard me from evil and the sins within my life that stand."
    He strove to God to proffer the glove of his right hand,
But from him was it taken by the Angel Gabriel.
The head of the Count Roland on his shoulder drooped and
fell!
His hands were crossed together as his end came over him;
But God hath sent unto him His holy cherubim.
Saint Michael-of-the-Peril-of-the-Sea was come likewise
With Gabriel, and Roland they bore up to Paradise.

CLXXIX. Roland is dead. His spirit hath God in Heaven
ta'en.
The Emperor to Roncevaux with the army came again.
Nor track, nor path, nor open space, nor grove, nor a foot
of ground
Was there but the dead Paynims and the dead Franks were
found.
    "Where art thou, fair my nephew?" loudly the Emperor
cried,

"And where is the Archbishop, and Count Olivier beside?
Gerier, Gerin, Othon and the Count Berengier?
And Ivoris and Ivo that are to me so dear?
What matter doth to Engelier of Gascony betide?
What hath befallen Samson and Anseïs full of pride?
Gerard the Lord of Roussillon, where may the old man be?
The twelve peers of the army that I left behind with thee?"
    What profits it? Was no one to answer and reply.
    "Christ God!" said the King Charlemagne, "In evil case am I
That I was not come hither what time they joined this war."
As a man in mighty anger his beard he plucked and tore
And sore he wept, and with him all the horsemen of the Franks.
There were twenty thousand on the ground that fainted in the ranks,
For whom exceeding pity did the Duke Neimes bear.

CLXXX. There was not any chevalier nor any baron there,
That for duty and for sorrow but was weeping without end,
For son and brother and nephew, for liege lord and for friend.
Upon the ground had fallen in a swound the greater part.
But now did the Duke Neimes like a man of gallant heart.
    "Two leagues from us look onwards," he, first of all, did say
To Charlemagne, "Thou mayst behold the dust rise in the way.
There is a host remaining yet to the Paynim foe.
March on, my master Charlemagne. Do thou avenge our woe."
    "God!" said the King, "Already are they far upon their flight.
Let every man strive to restore mine honor and my right.
Of the French realm the flower they have snatched it from mine hand."
    To Geboin and Otho the King gave his command
And to Tybalt of Rheims, moreover, and Milo the good Count.
    "Guard ye the field of battle, the valley and the mount.
Even as they fell in battle do ye now let them lie.
Unto them let no lion nor any beast draw nigh,
Nor squire, nor knave, nor any man shall to the place come near,

Until by God's good pleasure the host returneth here."
"Just Emperor! We will do thy will." They answered softly then
Of their great love. They kept with them a thousand of their men.

CLXXXI. King Charlemagne thereafter let all his trumpets blow.
Then forth with all the line of war did the great Emperor go.
Upon the traces of the foe then did the army fall.
In the hard chase of the Paynims they hastened one and all,
But when that night was coming on King Charlemagne had seen,
He alighted in a meadow upon the grasses green.
He bowed to earth. He prayed to God that the sun's course
He would stay,
That the night still might tarry and yet remain the day.
And lo! an angel that was wont to speak with him at hand.
Unto the Emperor Charlemagne swiftly he gave command.
"Charlemagne, march! In no way the light shall fail for thee.
God knoweth thou hast lost the flower of the Frankish chivalry.
Vengeance upon the caitiff race is given thee indeed."
When the Emperor had heard it, he leaped upon the steed.

CLXXXII. Now God for the King Charlemagne a miracle hath done,
For in the sky unmoving a space remained the sun.
The Paynims fled; the Frenchmen hard on their heels came on;
And in the Vale of Darkness they o'ertook them in their flight.
On to Saragossa they smote them in the fury of their might.
Ever the Franks marched slaying, dealing great strokes of wrath,
And they blocked up every highway and every bridle-path.
The Waters of the Ebro are before the foe at last.
Exceeding deep is the river and the current wondrous fast.
There was no barge, nor dromond, nor ferry by the shore.
Beseechingly the Paynims began straightway to implore
Termagant their god for succor. And therewith plunged they in

But in no way or fashion deliverance might they win.
Of them that were armed heavily at once a-many sank,
And many struck out vainly to reach the other bank.
Down stream some swam. The luckiest a deal of water drank
And in great pain and anguish they all were cast away.
Said the Franks: "Ye looked on Roland in a very evil day."

CLXXXIII. Then Charles looked on the Paynims that dead
lay all around,
Some that were slain in battle and the other moiety drowned.
His cavaliers much treasure in that hard fight had ta'en,
And the good King descended from off the steed again.
He bowed to earth and gramercy unto his God he said.
And when he rose from prayer at last the sun had fled.
Charlemagne spake:
                    "The hour for camping doth betide.
I deem that it is overlate to Roncevaux to ride.
Our steeds are worn and weary. Loose the bridle and the selle.
Let them rest them in the meadows."
                    Said the Franks: "Thou sayest well."

CLXXXIV. Twixt Valterne and the Ebro camped the
Emperor Charlemagne.
The Franks thereby dismounted in the middle of the plain.
They took the golden bridles and the saddles from the steeds.
Where was abundance of green grass they loosed them in
the meeds.
More they might not do for them. So weary was each wight
That he fell asleep upon the ground. No watch was set that
night.

CLXXXV. The Emperor in the meadow upon the earth him
laid.
Beside his head in that hour he put his mighty blade.
He would not in that night put off the armor that he bore.
The white-embroidered hauberk likewise the Emperor wore.
He had laced on the good helmet with the gold and jewels
brave.
He had girt on the sword Joyous—was never such a glaive;
And there shot thirty different hues each day from the great
sword.
We have heard of the lance that wounded upon the cross our
Lord.

By God His grace the spear-head was come to Charlemagne's
hand.
He had it wrought into the gold of the pommel of the brand.
For that glory and that goodness, Joyous the sword was
hight,
And it should not be forgotten of any Frankish knight,
For thereby the great battle-cry the shout Mountjoy have
they,
Wherefore no other nation may face them in the fray.

CLXXXVI. Clear was the night and the moon shone, and
the King lay down to rest;
But for Olivier and Roland grief lay heavy on his breast,
And the twelve peers and the Frenchmen in their blood at
Roncevaux.
Nor could he keep from weeping and sobbing in his woe
He prayed God to keep their spirits. He was weary from the
war,
For great had been his labor. He slept. He could no more.
And over all the meadows the Franks lay fast asleep.
There was no steed that longer upon his feet could keep.
An he wanted grass he cropped it, where'er he down had lain.
He hath learned a very mighty thing who understandeth
pain.

CLXXXVII. Charles slept like to a laborer with labor that
is spent;
And the Lord God Saint Gabriel unto the Emperor sent.
To watch beside King Charlemagne, God gave him His com-
mand.
And all night long by the King's head the angel took his
stand;
And he spake and told the Emperor in a vision of the night,
Concerning a great battle that against him they would fight.
And all the grievous meaning of the battle he made plain.
High up into the heavens looked the Emperor Charlemagne.
He saw the frost and the whirlwinds and the thunder where
they played,
The storms and wondrous tempests, and flames of fire arrayed.
And lo! upon his army fell that portent in a flash.
Afire were all the lances of apple-wood and ash,
And all the shields were flaming to the buckles of pure gold,
And likewise the good war-swords and the keen pikes mani-
fold.

And grated all the hauberks, and the steel helms ground
again.
His liegemen in their anguish appeared to Charlemagne.
Leopards were fain to eat them, and likewise many a bear.
Serpents and wiverns, dragons, and the foul fiends were there,
And thirty thousand gryphons. A fell attack they made
Upon the Franks that shouted: "King Charlemagne give
aid!"
And the heart of the Emperor was filled with pity and with
woe.
Fain had he gone, but there was that that would not let him
go.
Forth from a wood a lion came before him in his might.
Furious and full of pride was he and dreadful to the sight.
On the King's very body the lion leaped amain.
Locked arm by arm in the struggle wrestled and strove the
twain.
And none knew which should conquer, nor which of them
should fall.
The Emperor from his vision awakened not at all.

CLXXXVIII. Thereafter another vision was given him to
see.
At Aix in France beside a stair he deemed himself to be.
And the King thought by a double chain he held a mighty
bear;
And forth to him from Arden did thirty others fare.
Each spoke as a man speaketh. They said unto the King:
    "Sire, yield him now unto us. It is not a righteous thing
For thee to keep our kinsman. And we will aid him here."
    Then forth from out the palace a greyhound did appear.
On the green grass he grappled with the bear of greatest might
Before his mates, and Charlemagne beheld a marvellous fight.
But he knew not which should conquer and which should lose
the fray.
So much unto the hero God's angel did display.
Charles slept until the morning and the clear break of day.

CLXXXIX. His flight to Saragossa King Marsile good hath
made.
He dismounted from the charger 'neath an olive in the shade.
He hath pulled off the hauberk and the helmet and the sword.
And down he lay in disarray upon the fair green-sward.

His right hand had he lost, and cleft at the shoulder full in
twain
Was his right arm. He fainted from loss of blood and pain.
Bramimonde his wife before him wept and shrieked lament-
ing sore.
About the King were gathered thirty thousand men and
more.
Charlemagne and the sweet French realm they cursed them
all and one.
And then unto Apollo in his grotto did they run.
They heaped reproaches on him and many an evil name:
    "Ah, evil god! Now wherefore hast thou brought on us
this shame?
Why didst thou let our lord the King be beaten in the fight,
Who served thee well? And wherefore didst thou him so ill
requite?"
    Therewith his crown and sceptre from Apollo have they
ta'en.
By his hands unto a column they hanged him up amain.
Then in their wrath beneath their feet they trampled him
and trod,
And with great staves they beat him, and in pieces tore the
god.
His carbuncle from Termagant have the angry Paynims torn,
And they have hurled Mahomet into a foss forlorn.
The dogs devoured him, and the swine trampled him on the
ground.

CXC. At length hath the King Marsile awakened from his
swound.
Himself to his vaulted chamber he commanded them to bear.
Painting and colored writing a mighty store was there.
Tearing her locks Queen Bramimonde on her evil plight did
cry
With many tears. A word she spake in a loud voice and high:
    "How art thou, Saragossa, robbed and dispoiled this day
Of the great King and glorious who o'er thee bore the sway.
Our gods have played the traitor, who failed us utterly
In the fight this morn. The Amiral a coward will he be,
If he cometh not the battle with that fiery stock to bear,
That are so hardy-hearted that of life they have no care.
King Charlemagne the Emperor, with the great beard like a
flower,

Hath the rashness of great courage and all a hero's power.
Whereso'er he giveth battle, he never giveth way.
It is great woe that no one may be found that King to slay."

CXCI. Because of his good courage the Emperor Charle-
magne
Had been the full of seven year within the realm of Spain.
He had taken many a city, and, moreover, many a hold,
Wherefore was the King Marsile filled with trouble manifold.
And he let seal his letters ere the first year was spent,
And into Babylonia to Baligant he sent.
An ancient man was Baligant, of an old time and year.
Homer himself and Virgil were outlived of the Emir.
Marsile to Saragossa begged him his aid to bear.
And if he should not do it his gods he would forswear,
And all his idols also that his wont was to adore;
To Christianity the Holy, himself he would give o'er.
He was right fain with Charlemagne that a treaty should be
made,
For Baligant was far away and a great while had delayed.
To the men of his forty kingdoms gave Baligant command
His dromonds and his galleons to get ready to his hand,
And many a barge and pinnace, and ships of all degree.
There was at Alexandria a port upon the sea.
The Amiral got ready the ships of his array.
On the first day of summer, and in the month of May
The whole of his great armament embarked and went its way.

CXCII. Oh very great and mighty was that Paynim host of
war,
And they sailed very swiftly, and ever on they bore.
And set upon the yard-arms and at every main-mast head
Were carbuncles and lanterns that such a lustre shed
That, when was come the evening, the sea grew lovelier.
And when at last upon the coast of the Spanish land they
were,
Then all the land was lighted with the fire and the flame,
And the tidings of their coming to the King Marsile came.

CXCIII. That great host of the Paynims would in no way
stop or stay.
They left the salt sea waters. Into the fresh came they,

And Marbrise town and Marbros, they left them both
behind.
Up the channel of the Ebro did all that navy wind.
At the mast-head and the yard-arm was many a lantern-light
And carbuncle, great brightness that gave them in the night.
And unto Saragossa at day-break drew they on.

CXCIV. Then clearly broke the morning and brightly shone
the sun.
The Amiral from his galley came forth unto the land.
Beside him Espanelis walked on at his right hand.
Kings there were seen full seventeen that after him did fare.
Of counts and dukes I know not how many were come there.
And in the middle of the field under a laurel's shade,
On the green grass a tapestry of purest white was laid.
Thereon of the fair ivory was set a high-seat good,
Where Baligant the Paynim sate; but all the others stood.
And their Lord King unto them now made his meaning clear:
    "Ho, all ye free and gallant knights, now hearken and give
ear.
King Charles the Emperor of the Franks shall eat nor bite
nor sup
Till I have given my command to him to take it up.
He hath warred long in the land of Spain. But battle will I
give
To him in the sweet realm of France as long as I shall live,
Till he be dead, or a recreant hath yielded him to me."
    And with the glove of his right hand lightly he smote his
knee.

CXCV. When Baligant had said it, his will so strong had
grown
For all the gold beneath the heaven the King had not forgone
Marching on Aix, where justice was done by Charles the
King.
His henchmen when they heard it counseled likewise the
thing.
Clarien and Clarifan, two knights, he summoned to him
there:
    "Ye sons of the King Maltraien who was wont my word to
bear
With right good will; I bid you to Saragossa go,

And speak unto King Marsile that my coming he may know.
Against the Franks, in war-array have I come to succor him.
If I come on them, a battle there will be both great and grim.
Give him the glove gold-broidered. Do it on the King's right
hand
And give him this fine golden staff. When his duty for his land
He doth by me, to fight in France with Charlemagne will I
fare.
An he beg not mercy at my feet and Christian law forswear,
Then forthwith will I take away the crown from off his head."
    "Oh Sire, thou sayest wondrous well," thereto the Paynims
said.

CXCVI. To his messengers said Baligant:
                            "To ride doth you behove.
The staff let one now carry. Let the other bear the glove."
    And they answered him: "Dear master, we will even do
the same."
Then forth they rode so hard that they to Saragossa came.
Through ten gates have they ridden, o'er bridges four as well.
And all the street have they traversed wherein the burghers
dwell.
But when unto the summit of the city they drew near,
By the palace a great bruit fell loud upon their ear.
Enow of Paynims shrieked and wept and mighty woe
displayed.
Of their gods Mahound and Termagant a sore complaint
they made,
And moreover of Apollo, whence they got no help at all.
    Said each to each
                            "Unfortunate, what now shall us befall.
Confusion is upon us. Marsile from us is reft.
Through the hand of the King Marsile hath the Count
Roland cleft.
Nor have we left unto us even Jorfaleu the fair.
All Spain is theirs!"
                            The messengers dismounted at the stair.

CXCVII. Beneath an olive-tree got down those messengers
amain;
And two Saracens thereafter took from them their horses
twain.
And arm-in-arm together with their tidings on they went.

To the high part of the palace the two their footsteps bent.
Into the vaulted chamber they entered there above,
And their wicked salutation they gave there in all love:
   "Now may Mahound that ruleth us, and Apollo our good
lord
And Termagant protect the King, and the Queen watch and
ward."
   Said Bramimonde:
                        "Great folly now do I hear thee say.
Our gods are knaves. At Roncevaux most evil deeds did they.
They let of our true Paynims be slaughtered many a knight.
And my own dear Lord Marsile, they failed him in the fight.
The King's right hand is stricken off. Yea right hand hath
he none.
'Twas by the fierce Count Roland that the dreadful deed was
done.
King Charles will gain the whole of Spain. Ah, full of woe and
dread!
What will befall me? Woe is me, that none will strike me
dead."

CXCVIII. And Clarien answered:
                           "Lady, speak not so high and free.
Of Baligant the Paynim the messengers are we.
He saith he will ward King Marsile. He sendeth here beside
His staff and glove. In Ebro four thousand galleons ride,
And skiffs there be, and barges and galleys swift as well.
The number of the dromonds I know not how to tell.
The Amiral is stalwart and a great man of might,
And he will hasten into France with Charlemagne to fight.
And either will he slay him, or make him beg for grace."
   Said Bramimonde:
                     "The venture will be found in evil case.
The Amiral may lightly come on the Franks more near.
They have been here already the space of seven year.
The Emperor is gallant, of a great heart and high.
Ere from the field he flieth, in the battle he will die.
No King 'neath heaven, but Charlemagne deems him a babe
in worth.
The Emperor feareth no man that liveth on the earth."

CXCIX. And forthwith the King Marsile said unto her:
                                                  "Let be."

He spake unto the messengers: "Speak now, my lords, to me.
Ye see already I am doomed. Son or daughter, none remain,
Nor any heir, though one I had. Yestereven was he slain.
Bid my lord come and see me. He ruleth Spain of right.
An he desire I will yield it him, but for it let him fight
Against the French. Good counsel I will give him for the
fray
With Charlemagne that may be dead in a month's time from
this day.
With the keys of Saragossa to the Emir do ye hie!
Say to him, if he will trow me, that Charles will never fly."
    "Sire, thou hast spoken truly," did the messengers reply.

CC. And then said the King Marsile:
                            "The Emperor Charlemagne
Hath wasted all the country and my liegemen hath he slain.
And my cities he hath battered, and in their ruins laid.
For his army on the Ebro his camp-ground hath he made.
And from this city to that place but seven leagues there are.
Let the Amiral lead thither his mighty host of war.
Bid him for me for battle the gear of fight to don."
    The keys of Saragossa, he gave to them each one.
At that the two embassadors before the King bowed low.
They took their leave and at his word together did they go.

CCI. And thereon the embassadors got them upon the steed,
And forth out of the city they issued with all speed.
To their Emir they went in fear and gave to him amain
The keys of Saragossa. Spake the king unto the twain:
    "What have ye found! And Marsile that I summoned,
where is he?"
    And Clarien gave answer:
                                "He is wounded mortally.
Within the mountain passes was the Emperor yesterday.
For into the sweet land of France he yearned to take the
way.
And for the greater honor a rear-guard he arrayed.
Roland the Count his nephew there in the passes stayed,
And Olivier, and the twelve peers, and there beside them then
Of the land of France were gathered twenty thousand armèd
men.
And the King Marsile fought them like a good man of might.
He met with the Count Roland upon the field of fight.

With Durendal Count Roland such a buffet to him gave
That the right arm from his body with the same stroke he
clave.
And the son that the King held so dear hath Roland smitten
dead,
And all the barons likewise that to the fight he led.
King Marsile fled thereafter. Longer he might not bide.
And Charlemagne the Emperor hard on his heels did ride.
He bids thee aid him. He will yield to thee the realm of
Spain."
    Baligant thought. On madness was he like to come for pain.

CCII. "Sire Amiral," said Clarien, "In a fight yesterday
At Roncevaux Count Roland hath fallen in the fray,
And Olivier with the twelve peers that Charlemagne loved
well,
And twenty thousand Frenchmen in the same battle fell.
And, moreover, there his good right hand hath the King
Marsile lost.
Hotly the Emperor Charlemagne pursued after his host.
No longer are there cavaliers in all the country round
That are not slain in battle or in the Ebro drowned.
Camped are the Franks upon her banks; So near us have
they come
Into the land, but, an thou wish, hard is their journey home."
    Proud was the look of Baligant. His heart was glad and
high.
He rose up from the high-seat and loudly did he cry:
    "Tarry not, issue from the ships. To horse, ye barons bold,
And ride! Unless already King Charlemagne the old
Is stolen hence, this very day, for Marsile vengeance dread
Will I take, and for his reft right hand shall he have King
Charles his head."

CCIII. Those Paynims of Arabia out of their ships came
they;
The mules and steeds they mounted, and out they rode away.
What might they more? The Amiral, when he had sped
them all,
Gemalfin his companion unto himself did call:
    "I give into thy keeping the rule of all my power."
    Upon a great brown charger he mounted in that hour.
And thence together with him four mighty dukes he led,

And unto Saragossa without a halt they sped.
At the great stairs of marble they descended from their
mounts.
The stirrup of the Amiral was holden of four counts.
By the stairway of the palace they mounted up on high.
And Bramimonde came running:
                              "How miserable am I!
In what great shame my master is cast away!" she said,
"Charles' nephew hath confounded and smitten Marsile
dead."
    At his feet she fell. The Amiral hath raised her up again.
Unto the upper chamber in sorrow went the twain.

CCIV. When Marsile had seen Baligant, in a loud voice he
cried
Unto two Spanish Saracens, "Take me on either side
And raise me up." A gauntlet he took in his left hand.
Said Marsile:
                "My Lord Amiral, all of the Spanish land
I yield thee, and Saragossa and all that hangs thereby.
I have ruined all the people, and a ruined man am I."
    And Baligant gave answer:
                              "And therefore woe is me.
But now I cannot tarry to parley long with thee.
I know full well my coming is unknown to Charlemagne.
However, this same gauntlet I will take from thee again."
    And for the sorrow that he had, weeping he turned him
there.
Forth out of Marsile's palace he descended on the stair.
He rode so hard that forth he came before the foremost ranks,
Shouting as he came: "On, Paynims! Already flee the
Franks."

CCV. And early in the morning, when first the dawning
broke,
Then Charlemagne the Emperor from his deep sleep awoke.
Saint Gabriel, that by him for the guard of God had stayed,
Lifted his hand and o'er him the sacred sign he made.
Up rose the King and in that place he let his armor lie.
The others of the army likewise their arms put by.
And then to horse they got them and gallantly did ride
A long way on those mighty tracks and on the highroads wide.
Forth went the host to look upon that wondrous overthrow,
Where had been fought the battle in the pass at Roncevaux.

CCVI. Into the pass at Roncevaux entered King Charle-
magne.
And he began a-weeping when he found such store of slain.
He said unto the Frenchmen:
                              "Lords, ride not hastily,
For to go on before you it now behoveth me,
To seek him whom I yearn to find, even my nephew dear.
I was in Aix the city at a feast that fell each year.
There, of great fights and battles, their boasts my lads did
make.
And there I hearkened Roland and the matter that he spake;
If he e'er in the strange country should hap in fight to fall,
His comrades and his henchmen, he would excell them all;
Unto his foeman's country his last look would he bend;
Like a hero in his triumph he would come unto his end."
    Then, farther on than any a little stave might throw,
Up a hill before the army the Emperor did go.

CCVII. When forth to seek his nephew went the Emperor
Charlemagne,
Great store of herbs and flowers he found upon the plain,
The which the blood vermilion of our good lords did steep.
The King was filled with pity, nor could he choose but weep.
Under a tree high on the hill at last the Emperor drew.
The strokes of the Count Roland on the three steps he knew.
There he beheld his nephew on the green grass where he lay.
No marvel if the King was filled with anger and dismay.
He lighted from the horse and ran as swiftly as might be.
The body of Count Roland in his two arms took he.
Then he fainted on the body, so grievous was his pain.

CCVIII. Out of his swound awakened the Emperor Charle-
magne.
Count Accelin, Duke Neimes, Geoffrey of Anjou forby,
And Geoffrey's brother Thierry lifted the King on high,
They raised him underneath a pine, to earth his glance he
bowed.
And the King very gently began to mourn aloud:
    "Good Roland, in his mercy may the good God thee enfold.
So great a cavalier as thou never shall man behold,
To order and accomplish the great deed of the fight.
Now greatly doth mine honor go downward from the height."
    There swooned again King Charlemagne. He could not bear
the thing.

CCIX. At last out of his dreadful swound, woke Charlemagne the King.
There were four of the King's barons by the hands that held him high.
He looked to earth, and Roland beheld where he did lie.
Faded was the red. His body yet looked both fair and stark.
His eyes were turned within his head, and terrible and dark.
And Charlemagne wept for him in perfect faith and love:
    "Roland! God keep thy spirit in His place of flowers above.
Among the Saints of Heaven. How thou camest to ill in Spain!
Good Captain! not a day shall be but I shall suffer pain
For thee. My strength and courage are fallen in the sere.
No man is left unto me to keep mine honor clear.
Not a friend under heaven is left unto me now.
If I have any kinsmen, is none so brave as thou."
    And with both hands he tore his hair. So great their grief did grow,
Of an hundred thousand Frenchmen was none but wept for woe.

CCX. "Friend Roland, I will go to France. In Laon when I stand,
Within my chamber, strangers will come from many a land
They will ask for the Count-Captain; I will say he is dead in Spain.
In bitter sorrow thereafter in my kingdom shall I reign.
No day shall pass but I shall weep and groan aloud in ruth.

CCXI. "Roland! my friend! oh hero, and lovely in thy youth,
When I am in mine own chapel in the town of Aix once more,
Then men will come unto me asking tidings of the war,
And I will tell them tidings most marvellous and dread:
He who was wont to conquer, my nephew, he is dead.
Hereafter shall the Saxons rebel against my grace,
And the Huns and the Bulgarians and many another race,
The Romans and Apulians, and the men of Sicily,
And whosoe'er in Afric and Califerne there be.
And my suffering and sorrow shall grow from hour to hour.
What man can guide my army with such a strength and power
When he is dead that at the head thereof was wont to ride?
Ah! sweet my France, how utterly a waste thou shalt abide!
I have so great a sorrow to perish am I fain."

And then to rend his long white beard began King Charle-
magne,
And with both hands, moreover, to tear and pluck his hair.
A hundred thousand Frenchmen on the ground fainted there.

CCXII. "Friend Roland, great misfortune thy life has over-
cast,
Therefore thy gallant spirit to Paradise has passed.
Thy slayer all the land of France has smirched exceeding
sore.
I am so full of sorrow that I would live no more,
For the slaughter that upon my house because of me was
done.
But to God I make this prayer, to the Holy Virgin's Son:
Ere to the Sizré Passes in the mount I make my way,
May the spirit from my body depart from me this day.
With theirs may now this soul of mine be sent forth to
abide,
And may my flesh hereafter be forever them beside."
    Then he wept very greatly and plucked his beard again,
Said Duke Neimes: "Heavy sorrow is come on Charlemagne."

CCXIII. "Ah! grieve not so, Lord Emperor," Geoffrey of
Anjou said,
"But over all the field of fight let now search out our dead
That there were slain by them of Spain, and command them
to be borne
To a charnel-house."
              Then said the King: "Now blow upon thy horn."

CCXIV. And straightway Geoffrey of Anjou upon the horn
did sound.
Charles gave command. The Frenchmen descended to the
ground.
And all of their companions that they found in battle slain
Forthwith unto a charnel-house they carried them amain.
Of bishops and of abbots there was a mighty store,
Canons and clerks and parsons that tonsured foreheads bore.
And there they did absolve the dead and bless them in God's
name.
And myrrh and precious incense they lighted with the flame.
And gallantly they censed them and graved in noble kind.
Then—what more could they? forth they rode and left the
dead behind.

CCXV. A watch the Emperor Charlemagne set Roland's
body o'er,
And o'er the corpse of Olivier and of Turpin furthermore.
Likewise he there let open the bodies of the three,
And their three hearts, moreover, let wrap in cramoisy.
In caskets of white marble the hearts they then did lay.
The bodies of the barons they carried thence away.
They lapped them well in leather wrought of the red-deer
hide,
And with the wine and spices washed them and purified.
To Geboin and Tybalt and Count Milo spake the King,
And likewise Marquis Otho and commanded them this thing:
    "Onward in three chariots do ye now bear them forth."
    Well were the bodies covered with cloth of gold of worth.

CCXVI. Now was the Emperor Charlemagne set in his heart
to go.
When there arose before him the vanguards of the foe.
From the forefront of the army two messengers there came
For to denounce the battle in Baligant his name.
    "Proud King, it is not right nor meet that thou shouldst
now go back.
Behold the Emir Baligant, that rideth on thy track.
And mighty is that army that he leads from Araby.
This day shall we discover if there be strength in thee."
    King Charlemagne plucked at his beard. On the strange
overthrow
He thought, that came upon him in the fight at Roncevaux.
He looked proudly on his army. Then he cried with all his
force:
    "Arm you, ye Frankish barons, and straightway get to
horse."

CCXVII. The Emperor armed him foremost, and his hauberk,
swift did don,
And laced his helm, and Joyous the great sword girded on,
That bated not its brightness for the flaming of the sun.
And a Girondian buckler at his neck the King did hang.
He gripped his lance, and the good steel, he brandished it and
swang.
And thereupon he mounted on the great horse Tençendor
That at Marsonne by the river-ford he won, when he made
war

On Malpalin, the Narbonnese that by the King was slain.
And fierily he spurred the steed and loosed the bridle-rein.
Before an hundred thousand men at a gallop did he come,
Praising God and his Apostle, who hath his place in Rome.

CCXVIII. Down over that great meadow the men of France
did ride.
Were more than an hundred thousand that armed them side
by side.
Their armor well becomes them and swiftly run their steeds.
Fair are their spears. They get to horse and are ripe for gal-
lant deeds.
They deem there will be a battle, if they come upon the foe.
Down over their bright helmets the gonfalons hang low.
When King Charles had seen their faces how they were very
fair,
Then Josseran of Provence he summoned to him there,
Anthelm of Maintz and Neimes:
                                        "In such heroes as be here
A man should trust. He is a fool who giveth way to fear.
If their coming they repent not, dear shall the Arabs buy
Count Roland's death."
                    "God grant it us," said Neimes in reply.

CCXIX. Charles called Guinemant and Rabel:
                                        "To you I give command,
My lords, in the place of Roland and Olivier to stand.
One shall bear the sword, and the other, the mighty horn of
war.
At the head of the first legion do ye ride out before.
And fifteen thousand Frenchmen shall ride along with you,
The young men of the army, courageous youths and true.
And after you shall follow as many more beside;
And these shall the two marshals Geboin and Lawrence
guide."
    Count Josseran and Duke Neimes those columns did array.
If they come upon the Paynims there will be a fearful fray.

CCXX. French are the first two columns. When established
were the twain,
Of the vassals of Bavaria the third they did ordain.
The full of twenty thousand that troop was deemed to be.
There was not one among them that from a fight would flee.

Never a race neath heaven more dear the Emperor knew
Except for his own Frenchmen that the kingdoms overthrew.
They were led of the Dane Ogier, so well that loved the fight.
It was a gallant company of arrogance and might.

CCXXI. With Charlemagne already three lines of battle
stand.
And then the fourth Duke Neimes got ready to his hand
From a host of gallant barons that had great chivalry.
Germans they were, or gathered from the March of Germany.
Twenty thousand was their number by that all men did say.
Well armed were they and splendid were the steeds of their
array.
They flee no fight for fear of death, and Herman doth them
lead,
The Duke of Thrace, who will perish e'er he doth a coward's
deed.

CCXXII. Count Josseran and Duke Neimes forth the fifth
battle led.
They were twenty thousand Normans so all the Frenchmen
said.
And lovely is their armor, and their steeds are swift to run,
And ere they play the traitor they will perish every one.
Under heaven is no nation so much can undergo.
Richard the Ancient led them, that could smite so hard a
blow.

CCXXIII. The sixth array were Bretons and forty thousand
strong
Were the knights. Like gallant heroes on the steeds they rode
along.
Aloft they bore the lances. Laced were the flags of war.
The master of that army the name of Eudes bore.
But unto the Count Nivelon his place the man gave o'er,
And to Tybalt of Rheims and Otho the Marquis good beside:
    "A gift they are given to you. Do ye mine army guide."

CCXXIV. Now had the Emperor six brigades and the Duke
Neimes drew
The seventh up—the barons of Auvergne and of Poitou.
They might be forty thousand knights with steeds and
armour good.

Alone within a valley on a little hill they stood.
Charlemagne in benediction with his right hand made the
sign.
Count Josseran and Godselm were the marshals of that line.

CCXXV. And now the eighth, Duke Neimes established of
the bands
Of the barons of the Frisians and of the Netherlands.
Were more than forty thousand knights that battle would not
shun.
Then said the King: "By these indeed my service will be
done."
Twixt Rembolt and Count Hamon of Galicia there lay
The right to lead that army in courage through the fray.

CCXXVI. Duke Neimes and Count Josseran led the ninth
troop out amain,
The gallant men of Burgundy, the heroes of Lorraine.
And fifty thousand knights by count were there, laced helms
that wore
And hauberks good. Well-girded swords and twofold shields
they bore.
Strong are the spears, short-hafted. If the foe flee not away,
And if they join the battle, that host will smite to slay.
The Duke of Argonne, Thierry, was their captain for the fray.
And in the tenth good company was many a Frankish knight.
There were an hundred thousand of the best men of our
might.
And proud were all their faces, brawny their limbs appeared,
And like a flower was every head, and white was every beard.
In hauberk and double-byrnie every man of them was clad.
And great swords belted on them of France and Spain they
had.
And the bucklers that they carried bore many a cognizance.
Strong and staunch is every spear-shaft, and glorious every
lance.
They got to horse and shouted for the fight on every side,
And cried: "Mountjoy!" for Charlemagne along with them
did ride.
And onwards Geoffrey of Anjoy bore the great Oriflame—
Because it was Saint Peter's, it bore the Roman name.
But that they changed, and now Mountjoy on all lips it
became.

CCXXVIII. Down from his steed the Emperor got. On the
green grass did he kneel,
And turned him to the rising sun, and to God made his
appeal:
    "On this day, my very Father, do Thou aid me to prevail,
Thou who gavest Jonas succor in the belly of the whale,
Thou who the King of Nineveh of thy dear grace didst save,
And Daniel from the torment of the lions in the cave,
And in the fiery furnace didst protect the children three;
Upon this day of battle may Thy love be over me.
And if it please Thee, grant me, for Thy sweet mercy's sake,
For my dear nephew Roland great vengeance now to take."
    When he had done his orison on his feet he stood upright,
And signed upon his forehead the sign of wondrous might.
Upon his gallant charger he mounted with a spring;
And Josseran and Neimes held the stirrup for the King.
The King took up his buckler and his sharp cutting spear.
Fair and mighty was his body, and well did he appear.
And clear was all his countenance, and fierce he rode to war,
With the bellowing horns of battle behind him and before.
But the great horn of Roland was roaring over all.
And all the Franks were weeping for the sorrow of his fall.

CCXXIX. Fair rode King Charles. His mighty beard he
spread his armour o'er.
And so did all the army for the love to him they bore.
An hundred thousand Frenchmen might well be known there-
by.
The host came past the mountains and the cliffs that were so
high;
Through the deep clefts and dread defiles on did the army
haste;
And there at last they issued from the passes and the waste.
So took they their way onward into the March of Spain,
Until at last they halted in the middle of a plain.
The vanguard of the Amiral to Baligant they sped.
And unto him a Syrian among them rose and said:
    "We have seen the proud King Charlemagne. His men are
full of pride
They will not fail him. Arm you! For battle doth betide."
    Said Baligant:
                  "I hear a tale of mighty deeds renowned

That my men may understand it, let now the trumpets
sound."

CCXXX. Through all the host the tabors were sounded far
and near:
They blew upon the war-horns and on the trumpets clear
The Paynims all dismounted that their armour they might
don.
The Amiral brooked no delay. He got his byrnie on
With the broidered fringe, and laced the helm where bright
the good gold shone.
And then forthwith he girded the sword at his left side.
A name he had discovered for the great sword in his pride,
Because of the blade of Charlemagne whereof he heard the
fame,
And therefore "Precious" to the sword he had given for a
name.
And that within the battle was aye his rallying-call;
And evermore his cavaliers shouted it one and all.
About his neck thereafter a mighty shield he bound.
Golden was all the buckle with crystals set around.
And the cord was of the good red silk; and up he snatched
the spear.
Men called Maltêt. As huge and thick as a club did it appear.
The steel alone a burden for a mule had been indeed.
Forthwith the Emir Baligant hath mounted on his steed.
Marcules held his stirrup, the man from over sea.
The Amiral was splendid to behold in verity.
Great were his loins, and slim his flank, and broad and strong
his side,
Well wrought and fair his body. His chest was very wide.
Gigantic were his shoulders, and clear his glance and fair,
And haughty was his visage, and curling was his hair.
Even as a flower in summer his countenance was white.
He had proved him very often to be a man of might.
God! What a splendid hero, an a christened man he were.
He goaded till the blood ran clear his charger with the spur.
He ran his course, and o'er a trench with a great leap did he
ride.
Fifty feet was the measure thereof from side to side.
    Said the Paynims:
                    "Yonder Captain may well his marches hold.
Never is there a Frenchman that to joust with him is bold,

Or, will he not or will he, shall thereafter bide unslain.
When hence he did not flee away a fool was Charlemagne."

CCXXXI. Like a hero was the Emir. As a flower his beard
was white.
The wisdom of the Paynims he understood aright.
Arrogant was his spirit and furious in the fight.
Malprimis his son, moreover, was a hero of great mark,
Much like to his forefathers, and very stout and stark.
   "Sire, let us now ride onward," to his father then said he,
"For very much I wonder if Charles we e'er shall see."
   "Yea," said Baligant in answer, "his courage is so great.
The histories are many, his high deeds that relate.
But his strong nephew Roland he hath with him no more,
Nor will he have the courage to face us in the war."

CCXXXII. "Oh Malprimis, my own fair son," the Amiral
then said,
"Roland the gallant vassal yestreen was smitten dead.
And along with him, moreover, the courageous Olivier,
And all the twelve peers, also, whom Charlemagne held dear.
And there fell twenty thousand that were born on Frankish
earth.
But as for all the others a glove they are not worth.
Truly the Emperor cometh. My Syrian scout doth say
That into ten columns he hath marshalled his array.
Surely he is a gallant that the war-horn windeth so,
And clearly on the trumpet doth his companion blow.
And they twain march together before the foremost ranks.
And there are gathered with them full fifteen thousand
Franks
Of the young men that but children are held by Charlemagne.
There stride along behind them as many more again.
In great arrogance and anger will they march into the fight."
   Said Malprimis: "I pray thee; the first stroke let me
smite."

CCXXXIII. "Ah Malprimis my lovely son," gave answer
Baligant,
"Whatsoever thou desirest unto thee I will grant.
The assault against the Frenchmen now forthwith do thou
make.
But Torleu King of Persia for thy companion take,

And the Lord of Lithuania, King Dapamort, beside.
If haply thou mayst master the Emperor in his pride,
A portion of my kingdom to thee will I give o'er,
From Cheriant to Val Marquis."
                              "Now gramercy therefore."
Said Malprimis, and on he went to take within his hand
Earnest of the gift, that erewhile was the King Fleury's land.
But never will Prince Malprimis again his kingdom see.
The day of his investiture and seizin ne'er will be.

CCXXXIV. And Baligant the Amiral through the army rode
in state.
And Malprimis was at his heel that was so huge and great.
King Torleu and King Dapamort thirty columns did array,
And a very mighty legion of cavaliers had they.
The weakest of the columns is of thirty thousand men.
And first the men of Butentrot came out before them then,
Of whom was Judas that betrayed his God in sin and shame.
And after them the Milcians with the great heads there
came—
And their back-bones, moreover, have bristles like the swine.
The men of Blos and Nubians were marshalled third in line,
In the fourth did the Russians and the Slavonians ride.
In the fifth the men of Sobre and the men of Sor beside.
In the sixth did the Armenians and the Moriscos go.
And in the seventh battle were the men of Jericho.
In the eighth array were Negroes, in the ninth the Giants
stood.
The men of Balida the Strong, that never yet wished good,
Were in the tenth. The Amiral sware loudly as might be
By the body of Mahomet and his strength and majesty;
    "Like a fool cometh Charles of France. An he do not with-
hold
Battle will be. And nevermore shall he wear his crown of
gold."

CCXXXV. Thereafter ten great columns led forth the
marshals twain.
And the first of foul Orcanians in that hour did they ordain.
To march across Val Fui themselves they had bestirred.
The Turks made up the second host, and Persian was the
third.
And in the fourth was many a desperate Canaanite;

Of Soltras and of Avars was the fifth line of the fight.
In the sixth did the Ormalians and Euglians find place;
And in the seventh column were the men of Samuel's race;
And eighth and ninth the Prussians and Slavonians did stand.
Tenth came the men of Occiant, the waste deserted land.
They were indeed a nation who never served the Lord—
Never was race of villains yet heard of more abhorred.
Their hides are hard as iron; hauberk and helm therefore
They need not. They are cruel and desperate in war.

CCXXXVI. Forth Baligant the Amiral led other columns ten,
And the giant race of Malprose he ranked the foremost then.
Next came the Huns, and in third place came the Hungarian throng,
And in the fourth the army of Baldisa the Long.
From the dread Vale of Suffering the fifth brigade was come.
Sixth came whoe'er in Aiglent or Marmuse had his home.
The seventh line were Leians or of the land of Thrace.
The eighth of Argoille was, with them of Clarbone ninth in place.
And tenth and last of Val Fonde the bearded villains trod.
They were a folk that never had felt the love of God.
They numbered thirty columns in the history of the Franks.
Great were the hosts. The trumpets were sounding through the ranks.
And forth rode every Paynim most like a valiant knight.

CCXXXVII. Baligant the Amiral was a gallant man of might.
He had his Dragon borne before, and Termagant's ensign
And Mahomet's and the image of Apollo the Malign.
And gathered were ten Canaanites that marched along thereby,
And shouted out a mighty word in a loud voice and high:
    "Whosoever the protection of our Gods would now possess,
Let him now pray and serve them in sorrow and distress."
    And therewith all the heathen bent forward chin and brow.
And all their shining helmets in that hour did they bow.
    Then said the Franks:
                    "Ye villains! ye shall perish one and all.
This day a dire confusion upon your host shall fall.
And our God the Emperor Charlemagne will succor by his might,
And in the glory of His name shall we triumph in the fight."

CCXXXVIII. Baligant the Amiral is wise in many things.
To him his son he summoned and also the two Kings.
   "Do ye, my lords and barons, now forth before me ride.
All my columns of the battle do ye begin to guide.
But of the best of the columns three will I keep in hand.
The Turks and the Ormalians beside their King shall stand.
And of Malprose the Giants the third array shall be.
Also the men of Occiant shall march along with me.
With the Frenchmen and with Charlemagne they shall fight
the fearful fray.
If he fights me, from his shoulders will I cleave his head away.
Of that he may be certain. He deserves no other fate."

CCXXXIX. Beautiful were the lines of fight, and the hosts
were very great.
Between them was no mountain, nor little hill, nor dale,
Nor any copse or forest, that for refuge might avail.
Well they beheld each other across the open space,
And Baligant cried out aloud:
                              "Ho, warriors of my race,
Get you to horse and fiercely now in the fight fall on!"
   It was Amboire of Olifern who bore his gonfalon.
The Paynims yelled. On Precious the great sword shouted
they.
Said the Franks: "A mighty slaughter shall be done on you
this day."
And loud and high the battle cry Mountjoy they raised anew.
And by the Emperor's order all the horns of battle blew;
But bellowing over all men heard the horn of Roland blare.
   Said the Paynims then:
                              "The army of King Charles is
wondrous fair.
We are going to a battle most terrible and dread."

CCXL. The plain was very mighty and wide the country
spread.
Gigantic was the army that there its way did hold.
Glittering were all the helmets set with precious stones and
gold,
Broidered byrnies and laced pennons, and every shield and
spear.
And all the war-horns bellow and their voice is wondrous
clear.
And haughty is the sennet that they wind on Roland's horn.

The Amiral called to him Canabeu, his brother born,
That even to Val-Sevrée was the ruler of the land.
Unto Charlemagne's ten columns he pointed with the hand.
    "Behold the pride of famous France. Fierce rideth Charlemagne;
He cometh behind the foremost amid yon bearded train.
For down upon their hauberks they have let their beards
hang low,
And the beards of them are whiter than on the frost the snow.
With the blades and with the lances the great strokes will
they smite.
We are like to have a dreadful and a very desperate fight.
Never a man the like has seen on any stricken field."
    Then farther than a man might cast a cudgel cleanly
peeled
Baligant went before his men. His mind he spake and
showed:
    "Ho, Paynims! follow after, for I will clear the road."
And the spear he shook it greatly and brandished it again.
And he turned thereof the iron head against King Charlemagne.

CCXLI. But when the Emperor Charlemagne the Amiral
surveyed,
And the Dragon and the ensign and the standard there displayed,
And the soldiers of Arabia whereof such store came on—
All the quarters of the country their host had overrun,
Save that where with his army did the Emperor abide—
The King of France right loudly lifted up his voice and cried:
    "Lords of France a-many stricken fights have ye fought
and ye are brave.
Behold the Paynims. Every one is a coward and a knave.
Their whole faith is not worth a groat; though great their
army be,
What boots it? Who will charge them, let him now come with
me."
Forthwith with the good rowels he spurred the charger there,
And Tençendor the charger leaped four times in the air.
    "This our King is a good hero," forthwith the Frenchmen
said,
"No man of us will fail thee. Gallop on, Lord King, ahead."

CCXLII. On high the sun was shining, and lovely was the day,
Beautiful were the armies and gigantic each array.
And now the foremost ranks thereof in battle met amain.
Count Rabel and Count Guinemant to their fleet steeds gave the rein.
And out they spurred with all their speed and the Franks with one accord
Spurred after them, and came to fight with the sharp edge of the sword.

CCXLIII. Count Rabel was a cavalier of a great heart and bold.
He spurred on the war-charger with the spurs of the fine gold.
Torleu the King of Persia he rode to overthrow.
His buckler and his byrnic might not abide the blow.
Through the man's body, of the spear was thrust the golden head.
Over a little thicket he smote the Paynim dead.
Said the Franks
            "May God Almighty now aid us to prevail.
For the right is with King Charlemagne, and him we cannot fail."

CCXLIV. And now against the Lettish King, Guinemant fought the fight.
All of his flowery buckler in pieces did he smite,
And shattered all the byrnie. And furthermore he ran
His gonfalon right through the midst of the body of the man.
He struck him dead most certainly whether for mirth or woe.
And forthwith all the Frenchmen raised a great shout at the blow.
    "Smite, Lords! Stay not! For a just cause against the Paynim race
Hath our King. And God hath set us in His very judgment place."

CCXLV. On a white steed sate Malprimis. Through the press of Franks he bore,
Dealing out a goodly measure of the great strokes of war.
Each over each the dead men he smote down on every side.
Then first the Emir Baligant lifted his voice and cried:

"To nourish you, my barons, long time I have been fain.
My son now see how eagerly he seeketh Charlemagne,
And so great a store of barons defieth unto fight.
I will never ask for vassal of better heart and might.
Go now and bear him succor with the sharp point of the
lance."
    And with that word the Paynims to battle did advance.
Hard are the strokes and fierce the fray. 'Tis a battle won-
drous sore
A keener fight was never fought since that time or before.

CCXLVI. O angry are the armies! Wide are the hosts and
large.
And now have all the columns encountered at the charge.
And wondrously the Paynims went striking stroke on stroke.
God's name! How many lances in pieces twain they broke,
And shields burst, and from byrnies rent all the mail away.
There mightest thou see how scattered on the field the bodies
lay.
And the whole field of battle with the fine green herbage
strown
With the blood out of those bodies was all vermilion grown.
And once again the Amiral cried out unto his train:
    "Ho! now upon these Christians, my barons, smite amain."
Hard and fearful was the battle. The like was never kenned
Since or before. Nor ends it until death shall make an end.

CCXLVII. "Smite Paynims! Ye are come for that," to his
men called the Emir,
"And I will give you women both beautiful and dear.
Fiefs and lands will I give you, and possessions fair and wide."
"To smite is our whole duty," the Paynim host replied.
At the first stroke all their lances were shivered in their hands.
Then forth they drew together an hundred thousand brands.
There had you had a sorrowful and terrible mellay.
Whoe'er therein would enter might behold a dreadful fray.

CCXLVIII. The Emperor besought the Franks:
                          "Lord barons, verily
I love and trust you. Ye have fought so many fights for me,
And ta'en so many kingdoms, and great kings overthrown,
And that I owe you guerdon to me is right well known—
The guerdon of my body and my lands and my domain.

Now for them do ye take vengeance that yesterday were
slain—
Your sons and heirs and brothers in the pass at Roncevaux.
Right well ye wot yours is the right against the Paynim foe."
   "Lord King! Thou speakest truly," the Frankish host
replied.
There were twenty thousand of them that with Charlemagne
did ride.
And all of them together unto him gave their faith
That never would they fail him for danger or for death.
Was none that played not with the spear. But right soon did
they smite
With the keen sword; and grievous and dreadful waxed the
fight.

CCXLIX. Now Malprimis the baron galloped hard amid the
fray.
A many of the Frenchmen it fortuned him to slay.
Neimes the Duke beheld him and his look was full of pride.
Like a man of mighty courage against him did he ride.
The high boss out of the buckler with a fearful blow he smote,
And the embroidered coverings twain, he rent from the mail-
coat.
Right through the Prince's body his golden banner bore.
He smote him dead seven hundred of his servitors before.

CCL. The brother of the Amiral, King Canabeu was he.
Straightway the battle charger he spurred forward furiously.
He drew his blade—the hilt was set with crystals all a-row.
On Neimes' princely helmet he struck a fearful blow.
And the half thereof the Saracen did sorely rend and rive.
With the sharp edge of the warsword he cut through laces
five.
The iron plate above his brow a groat it was not worth.
To the skin the Paynim clove the coif, and a fragment fell to
earth.
Fierce was the stroke, and sorely the Duke it did astound.
If God had not sustained him, he had fallen to the ground.
He gripped the neck of the charger. If the foeman smite again.
Dead is the noble vassal. To his aid ran Charlemagne.

CCLI. And the Duke Neimes suffered great agony and woe,
And Canabeu the Paynim ran in to lay him low,

Said Charlemagne: "Thou dastard! an ill stroke didst thou
smite."
And forth he rushed against him in the fury of his might.
The buckler of that Paynim he crushed against his heart.
The neck-joint of the hauberk he rended it apart.
And through the caitiff's body he thrust the lance right well,
That he smote him dead. And empty thereafter was his selle.

CCLII. And very heavy sorrow King Charlemagne came o'er,
When he beheld Duke Neimes before him wounded sore,
And how from the Duke's helmet the clear blood spouted free.
The Emperor spake his counsel:
                                        "Ride hither unto me,
Neimes, fair lord. The scoundrel that hath wrought thee this
mischance
Is dead, and I have once for all transfixed him with my lance."
    Neimes the Duke gave answer:
                                        "I trow it master mine;
And, if I live hereafter, great profit shall be thine."
    "In love and faith together they hastened onwards then.
The Franks that marched beside them were twenty thousand
men.
Was none but smote and fiercely stroke upon great stroke
laid.

CCLIII. Baligant through the battle, on his steed his way
he made.
And in his hand he carried the spear both sharp and strong.
To smite against Count Guinemant, he galloped hard along.
And against the heart he shattered the hero's buckler white.
The broideries of the hauberk he tore them left and right.
From side to side he severed the hero's flanks in twain.
From the back of the fleet charger he hurled to earth the
slain.
Then Baligant Lord Geboin and Lawrence overthrew,
And Richard the Old, the Captain, of Normandy he slew.
    The Paynims cried:
                                "Most wondrous is Precious the great glaive.
Smite, barons! In the warsword is that which shall us save."

CCLIV. 'Twas a great sight to look upon, that Arab host of
war—
Men of Occiant and of Argoille and the Biscayan Shore.

Well enow with the long lances against the Franks they
drove,
But now to yield to them the field the Frenchmen did not
love.
There were a very many that fell on either side;
And furiously the battle went on till vespertide.
The barons of the Frankish host a mighty loss had they.
There was enough of sorrow ere the ending of the day.

CCLV. Fiercely against each other did the Franks and Pay-
nims strike.
They shivered many lances, and many a burnished pike.
Whoso saw the bucklers shattered, or heard the fearful
crash
Of the white mail, or the warswords on the helmets that did
clash;
Or whoso saw the cavaliers on every side that fell,
And hearkened of the dying on the ground the wail and yell,
Might keep within his spirit a memory of woe.
It was indeed a battle that was hard to undergo.
To Apollo and Mahomet and Termagant each one
    Cried the Emir:
                    "Ah, my lord gods! your service have I done
But over well. Your images shall of fine gold be made.
Against the Emperor Charlemagne protect me and bear aid."
    But now his friend Gemalfin came forth before the King
Very evil were the tidings that with him he did bring.
    He cried
            "Lord Baligant, this day ill hast thou led the host,
For thy son Malprimis to thee among the foes is lost.
And Canabeu thy brother is slaughtered in the fray.
And for the two French champions fairly hath gone the day.
That one was the King Charlemagne most certainly I deem.
Big-bodied like a warden of the marches did he seem.
His beard is white as an April flower." Baligant bowed the
helm,
And thereafter hid his visage. Such grief did overwhelm
The Emir that he thought forthwith to die of misery.
Jangleu he summoned to him, the man from oversea.

CCLVI. "Ho Jangleu," said the Amiral, "Stand forth before
me now.
Exceeding great is thy wisdom, and a gallant man art thou.

By thy counsels at all seasons 'tis my custom to abide
Betwixt the Franks and Arabs what think'st thou shall betide?
Shall we triumph in this battle?"

                                The other answer gave:
   "Dead art thou, Baligant! Thy gods thy life they cannot save.
Brave is King Charles and gallant are all his men of war.
So fierce a race of fighters I have not seen before.
But now the knights of Occiant and the Turks do thou command,
Enfrons, Arabians, Giants now gather to thy hand.
Delay no more the matter that thou shouldst be about."

CCLVII. His beard above his byrnie the Amiral shook out;
As any hawthorn-flower the goodly beard was white.
Whate'er befel, in no way would he hide him in the fight.
And to his mouth thereafter he set a trumpet clear.
And loud he blew upon it that the heathen host might hear.
And through the field of battle he rallied his array.
Loud did the men of Occiant in answer bray and neigh,
And all the men of Argoille like dogs did yelp and bark.
They fell upon the Frenchmen in very madness stark.
Right through the thickest of them the Paynims burst and broke,
And a full seven thousand fell dead before their stroke.

CCLVIII. Never had the Count Ogier been touched by dread or fear.
Than he a better vassal ne'er put on battle-gear.
When he beheld the columns of the Frenchmen broken through,
To Thierry Duke of Argonne and to Geoffrey of Anjou
And Count Josseran he shouted. Proudly to Charlemagne
He spake:
             "Of these same Paynims see how thy men are slain.
In God's sight, 'twill not be pleasing that thy head should wear a crown,
If so be it that thou smit'st not to avenge this ill-renown."

   They said no word but hard they spurred; they let the horses go,
And went to smite wherever they might come upon the foe.

CCLIX. Ogier the Dane and Charlemagne well the great strokes laid on,
And Neimes and Geoffrey of Anjou that bore the gonfalon.
Ogier the Dane in all things a hero good was he.
He spurred the steed beneath him, and let him gallop free.
On him who bore the Dragon he let drive a buffet dread.
Down to the earth before him he hurled Lord Amboire dead.
And the banner of King Baligant in that hour came to ground.
And Baligant beheld it fall, and the ensign of Mahound
Without a man to guard it. In his heart he saw it plain
How wickedness was on his side and the right with Charlemagne.
Those Paynims of Arabia less furiously did ride,
And the Emperor raised up his voice, and to the Frenchmen cried:
    "Speak, lords! Will ye aid me for God's love?" The Franks their answer gave:
    "Thou askest ill. Who smites not with his whole strength is a knave."

CCLX. Now all the day passed over, and nearer came the night.
The Frenchmen and the Paynims with the sword they fought the fight.
They were very gallant captains that joined those hosts of war.
The memory of their war-cries they had not given o'er.
Baligant called on Precious, but the far-famed cry
Mountjoy cried Charles. And each knew each by the clear voice and high.
And now those two encountered amidmost of the field,
And charged, and either other smote upon the rose-wrought shield
With the lances. And the targets broke beneath the buckles wide.
The fringes of the hauberks they rended from the side.
Neither pierced the other's body, but either broke his girth.
The saddles turned. They staggered, and fell unto the earth.
To their feet very swiftly arose those angry lords,
And in most gallant manner they got them to their swords.
There cannot be an ending hereafter of this fray.
They cannot cease from battle till one the other slay.

CCLXI. A gallant man was Charles of France, the lovely land
and dear.
In no way did the Amiral feel any doubt or fear.
And either of the heroes lifted up the naked glaive.
On the shield each to the other the dreadful buffets gave.
And they cut through the two-fold wood and through the
folds of hide.
Flew the nails, and into pieces fell the buckles far and wide.
Then smiting on the hauberks breast against breast they
came.
Out of the fiery helmets flew up the sparks of flame.
So furious a battle could not endure for long.
Behoved one or the other there to confess his wrong.

CCLXII. Said Baligant:
                    "King Charlemagne look well to thine intent.
Take counsel of thy wickedness unto me to repent.
My son within the battle I deem that thou didst slay.
And wrongly now thou seekest my realm to take away.
Become my liegeman; for a fief I will give my realm to thee.
From here unto the Orient my vassal shalt thou be."
    And Charlemagne gave answer:
                            "Right evil words are these.
I owe not to a Paynim either true love or peace.
Receive now the salvation given of God above,
Even the law of Jesus Christ, and thee I still will love.
Serve and trust the King Almighty!"
                            "Yon are most evil words,"
Said Baligant. Then fell they on with the keen cutting
swords.

CCLXIII. The Amiral in all things was of excelling might,
And through the brown steel helmet of the Emperor did he
smite.
Upon his head the helmet was broken through and rent.
Even through the fine locks of his hair fell the blade in its
descent.
Of flesh a handsbreadth good and more away the sword did
tear.
On the place whereon it lighted, naked was the bone and bare.
Reeling and near to falling was the King Charlemagne.
But God willed not in that hour that he should be ta'en or
slain.

And then unto the Emperor in haste Saint Gabriel sped.
 "What dost thou, King most mighty?" to him the angel
said.

CCLXIV. When of the holy angel Charlemagne the voice
did hear,
He had no dread of dying, and knew not any fear.
And strength of mind and body anew in him awoke.
On the Emir with the blade of France he smote a dreadful
stroke.
The helm where flamed the jewels with that buffet did he
crush,
He clove the head in sunder, and out the brains did gush;
And straight through the man's visage to the beard that was
so white
Beyond all hope or question stone dead he did him smite.
And that his men might know him, "Mountjoy!" he shouted
high.
At the word Duke Neimes hastened and to the King drew
nigh,
And brought the steed. King Charlemagne leaped upon
Tençendor.
The Paynims turned. God would not that they should tarry
more.
And now the Franks have won the boon for which they had
implored.

CCLXV. The Paynims fled according to the will of God the
Lord.
The Franks pursued, and with them the Emperor did go.
Spake the King:
          "Ho now, my barons! Take vengeance for your woe.
Achieve your whole desire, and in your hearts be glad,
For it was but this morning I beheld you weeping sad."
    Said the Franks:
            "Sire, let us do the deed." And each began to slay,
Even as he might. But a remnant of the Paynims got away.

CCLXVI. Fierce was the heat and clouds of dust rose up-
ward to the height,
And the Franks pressed the Paynims most fiercely in their
flight—
Even unto Saragossa the pursuit did not relent.

To the summit of her tower Queen Bramimonde she went.
And clerks and priests of the false law God loves not with her
sped.
They have no ordination or tonsure on the head.
When she beheld the Arabs into such confusion thrown,
She hastened unto Marsile, and shrieking made it known:
  "Mahomet aid! Ah, gentle King, our host is smitten amain,
And in very great dishonor the Amiral is slain."
  When Marsile heard the tidings he turned unto the wall,
And hid his face, and bitterly his tears began to fall.
Weighed down with sin and shamefulness he died there of
his dole,
And the eternal fiends of Hell got hold upon his soul.

CCLXVII. Thus slain were all the Paynims, save those who
fled away,
And Charlemagne the Emperor hath conquered in the
fray.
In Saragossa city the gates were battered down;
But the Emperor knew surely that defenceless was the town.
He took the place. He entered with his war-host in his might.
There the King and all his army laid him down to sleep that
night.
Exceeding proud was Charlemagne with the white beard in
that hour.
Queen Bramimonde surrendered unto him every tower.
There ten great towers and fifty of lesser note did stand.
Well endeth his adventure that is succored of God's hand.

CCLXVIII. And now the day was over, and on the night-
time came.
And clear the moon was shining, and the stars were flashing
flame.
The King had ta'en Saragossa. A thousand men around
He bade march through town and temple and the mansions of
Mahound.
With the axes that they carried, and with the iron maul,
They smote Mahound, and shattered his idols one and all,
That sorcery and falsehood, no longer might remain.
The King loved God. His service to accomplish was he fain.
The bishops blessed the water. The Paynims did they bring
To baptism. And if any held out against the King,
Or burned, or hanged, or slaughtered with the sharp sword
was he then.

At that time were there baptizèd an hundred thousand men,
True Christians all; all save the Queen that captive did depart
To lovely France. The King desired God's love should change her heart.

CCLXIX. And the long night passed over, and brightly broke the day.
Charles garrisoned the towers with the men of his array,
He left a thousand cavaliers behind him proved and bold,
In the Emperor's name the city to govern and to hold.
And the King and all his barons got quickly on the steed,
And Bramimonde, a captive, in the army did they lead,
But he intended nothing save good unto the dame.
In gallantry and glory along their way they came.
In their strength and in their power they passed Narbonne the town,
And hastened unto Bordeaux the city of renown.
And there upon the altar of brave Saint Severin's shrine
He set the horn of Roland filled with golden pieces fine.
The pilgrims have beheld it that to the place have gone.
He passed the Gironde river in the great ships thereon.
Unto Blaye he brought his nephew, likewise his comrade good,
Even Olivier, and Turpin that had such hardihood
And wisdom. And he laid the lords in sepulchres of white.
In the church of Saint Romanus lieth each gallant knight.
To God and the Holy Names the Franks their spirits did commend.
Through the mountains and the valley King Charlemagne did wend.
For nothing would he tarry till he came to Aix the town.
He rode till at his stairway from the charger he got down.
And when at last the King was come into his high-built hall
Forthwith he summoned to him his judges one and all,
From Bavaria and Saxony and Friesland and Lorraine.
He summoned them of Burgundy, and them of Alamain,
Poitevins, Normans, Bretons, and every wisest man
In the realm of France, and the trial of Ganelon began.

CCLXX. Back from the Spanish Marches returned King Charlemagne
To Aix the fairest city in the land of France again.
He mounted in his palace unto his chamber fair,

And Aude the lovely lady came forth unto him there.
She spake unto the Emperor:
                "Count Roland where is he,
That to take me for his wedded wife plighted his troth to
me?"
   And Charles was filled with sorrow and heaviness of heart.
He plucked his beard, and from his eyes the tears began to
start:
   "Thou askest me, dear sister, of one that doth not live.
Another and a better unto thee I will give.
It is Louis—and a better there is not found in France.
He is my son, and my domains are his inheritance."
   And Aude replied unto him:
                "What monstrous words are these!
God and His Saints and Angels in no way would it please
That after Roland's passing I yet on earth should dwell."
   Her color fled and suddenly at the King's feet she fell,
And perished. Now her spirit God in His grace receive!
Wept all the Frankish barons and sorely did they grieve.

CCLXXI. Now Lady Aude the beautiful the end of life had
found.
The Emperor thought within him that she was but in a
swound,
And his heart was filled with pity, and sore he wept for pain,
And in his arms he took her, and raised her up again.
But aye upon her shoulders drooped the fair lady's head.
And when the King beheld it that she verily was dead,
Four countesses he summoned. To a nunnery was she borne.
And all the night they watched her till the breaking of the
morn.
And underneath an altar they wrought her sepulchre,
And with exceeding honor the King let bury her.

CCLXXII. Now to Aix returned the Emperor. Ganelon the
traitor hound
Was there before the palace in chains of iron bound.
There to a stake that villain in shameful guise they tied.
His hands were girded stoutly with thongs of red-deer hide.
And nobly did they beat him with an ox-yoke and the stave.
But he deserved no other than the measure that they gave.
So in exceeding anguish for his trial did he wait.

CCLXXIII. It is written in the ancient book these deeds that
doth relate
That Charlemagne unto him men of many lands did call.
At Aix within the chapel they gathered one and all.
The feast was very glorious. It was the holy day
Of Saint Silvester the good lord, by that which many say.
And then began the trial, and abroad did rumor run
Concerning Ganelon the Count the treason that had done.
The Emperor before him the prisoner bade them bring.

CCLXXIV. "Lord barons," to the judges said Charlemagne
the King,
"Concerning the Count Ganelon make now a just decree.
He marched amid mine army to the land of Spain with me.
And twenty thousand Frenchmen he caused them to be slain,
And Roland my good nephew whom ye ne'er shall see again,
And Olivier, moreover, the courteous and the bold,
And the twelve peers this traitor for filthy lucre sold."
    Said Ganelon:
                "An I gainsaid, I would be a traitor strong.
But in gold and in possession Roland did me grievous wrong.
Therefore did I desire his death and his distress;
But that the thing was treason I never will confess."
    Said the Franks in answer: "Counsel we now will take
thereon."

CCLXXV. Before the King there might ye see the great
Count Ganelon.
And gallant was his body, and his face was fair of hue.
Well had he been a baron good, had he been leal and true.
On the Franks and on the judges Ganelon turned his eye,
And on thirty of his kinsmen that unto him stood nigh.
And then in a loud voice and high unto them he did shout:
    "For the love of God I pray you, ye barons, hear me out.
I was in the King's army and served him faithfully
And in all love. But Roland his nephew hated me.
And therewithal he plotted how in great pain I should die.
Therefore unto King Marsile embassador was I,
And only by my wisdom did I hap my life to save.
And I defied Count Roland, the stalwart and the brave.
And Olivier and likewise, all the comrades of their train—
These noble barons heard it, and the King Charlemagne—

I venged myself. But treason—I wot it was not so."
    And the Franks spake in answer: "To counsel let us go."

CCLXXVI. When Ganelon saw his trial how it began apace,
There were thirty of his kinsmen that he summoned in the
place.
And one there was to whose command the others hearkened
well.
From Sorence the fair castle was the Lord Pinabel.
Well could he talk and clearly speak forth his thought aright.
And he was brave and skillful with his weapons in the fight.
    "I trust thee, friend," unto him Count Ganelon did say,
"Free me from this shame of trial and the risk of death
this day."
    And Pinabel gave answer:
                              "Well defended shalt thou be.
Nor is there any Frenchmen that to hang condemneth thee,
(If the Emperor to fight the man will grant me and accord)
But I will give the lie to him with the sharp edge of the
sword."
    And at the feet of Pinabel fell the Count Ganelon.

CCLXXVII. The Bavarians and Saxons to the Council got
them gone.
There were Franks and men of Normandy and likewise of
Poitou.
And of Germans and Thediscans a-many thither drew.
They of Auvergne were soft of heart. Because of Pinabel
They kept them close. Said each to each:
                              "To let it rest were well.
Let close the trial; to Charlemagne now let us make this
prayer
That Ganelon acquitted for this time he declare.
Let him then serve the Emperor in true love and in faith.
Ye will never see Count Roland, for his head is low in death.
For gold and gear he cannot bring back the Marquis more.
'Tis a fool that undertaketh to take up this gage of war."
    Was none within the Council but granted it was true
Save Thierry that was brother of Lord Geoffrey of Anjou.

CCLXXVIII. The barons went to Charlemagne, and said:
                              "Sire, hear our prayer.
Count Ganelon acquitted for this time do thou declare.

And do thou let him serve thee in true love faithfully.
Give him his life, for certainly a goodly man is he.
Roland is dead. Upon him we shall not look again.
Nor win him back with treasure."

Then the King Charlemagne
Answered and said unto them: "Ye are villains all indeed."

CCLXXIX. When the King saw that all of them had failed
him in his need,
Then his countenance and visage on his breast he bended low,
And called himself a caitiff in the torment of his woe.
But lo! the good knight Thierry unto the King he drew,
Even he that was the brother of Duke Geoffrey of Anjou;
Lean was the man of body, and exceeding thin and spare.
And dark was Thierry's countenance, and coal-black was his
hair.
Not over large in stature, nor yet of little height.
He spake unto the Emperor like a very courteous knight:
    "My fair Lord King, now let not thine anger rise so strong.
Thou knowest well already that I have served thee long.
This trial in my forbears' right is mine to pass upon.
Whatsoever the Count Roland did unto Ganelon,
Thy service should have been to him a strong defence and aid,
And a traitor is Count Ganelon, that Roland thus betrayed.
He has perjured him before thee, and treason wrought most
high.
Therefore it is my judgment that he be hanged and die,
And that his body also suffer shame and torture both,
Like unto any traitor a villainy that doth.
And if to me shall give the lie a kinsman of his blood,
With the blade that I have girded will I make my judgment
good."
And all the Franks gave answer: "Now hast thou spoken
well."

CCLXXX. Now unto the King Charlemagne came forward
Pinabel.
Great was the man, and mighty, and swift and strong in war.
And he to whom he dealt a stroke, his time of life was o'er.
He said unto the Emperor:
                "This trial is for thee,
Oh King; give orders straightway that no more tumult be.
Thierry hath given judgment. I say that he has lied;
I will fight."

He put on his right fist the glove of red-deer hide.
Said the King then:
                    "The hostages of the trial give me now."
Therewith the thirty kinsmen gave in their pledge and vow.
  "I will give thee pledges also," said the Emperor thereon,
And he caused them to be guarded till justice should be done.

CCLXXXI. When Thierry well had seen it that the fight he
soon must wage,
He gave unto the Emperor his right-hand glove for gage.
And pledges for his warrant the Emperor gave o'er.
And at the word of Charlemagne they brought in benches
four;
And thereon did they seat them who were to fight the fight.
In the eyes of all men present is the trial meet and right—
Ogier it was of Denmark that for all this took heed.
And now each champion shouted for his armor and his steed.

CCLXXXII. When at last unto the battle within the lists
they came,
Well they confessed and were absolved and blessed in God
His name,
And Mass they heard, and also Communion did receive,
And to the monasteries great offerings did they leave.
Forth went the twain to Charlemagne. On the heel was set
the spur.
They wore the milk-white hauberks, so light and strong that
were.
Their helmets shut and shining their faces did enfold.
Their swords were girded on them with hilts of the pure gold.
About their necks the champions their quartered bucklers
wore,
And likewise in their good right hands the sharpened lances
bore.
And thereupon they mounted on the chargers swift and
proud.
An hundred thousand cavaliers began to weep aloud,
Who because of the Count Roland were sad for Thierry's
sake.
God knoweth thereof certainly what end the fight will take.

CCLXXXIII. Hard under Aix the city there is a mighty lea,
And there of the two barons the battle was to be.

Gallant were both the heroes, and fleet the chargers twain.
And either champion spurred his steed, and dropped his
bridle-rein.
In valor and great courage, each against the other dashed.
Right through the rival bucklers the rushing lances crashed.
And broken were the hauberks, and broken either girth.
The cantels of the saddles fell down unto the earth,
There were an hundred thousand wept loudly at this sight.

CCLXXXIV. Now unto earth hath fallen from his charger
either knight.
And forthwith very swiftly they got them to their feet.
A stalwart man was Pinabel, and a very light and fleet.
And the one sought out the other; no chargers needed they.
With the blades with hilts of the pure gold they smote and
hacked away,
On the steel helms. And the great strokes the helms were like
to cleave.
And loud the Frankish cavaliers because of it did grieve.
"Ah God," said the King Charlemagne, "The right now
make it known."

CCLXXXV. Said Pinabel:
                    "Ho, Thierry, thine error do thou own.
In true love and in honor thy liegeman will I be.
I will give my whole possession at thy pleasure unto thee.
But the peace of the Count Ganelon with the Emperor do
thou make."
    And Thierry answered:
                    "Never such a counsel will I take.
If I did it, for a villain would I evermore be ta'en.
But God shall make His judgment this day between us twain.

CCLXXXVI. Said Thierry:
                    "A good baron art thou, O Pinabel.
Thy strength is great exceeding, and thy body fashioned well.
And all thy peers have known thee for a very valiant knight.
But do thou now give over from fighting out the fight.
With the King will I accord thee. On Ganelon shall they
wreak
Such vengeance, not a day shall pass but men thereof shall
speak."
    And Pinabel gave answer:

          "God's will is not therein.
I will not cease to comfort and to sustain my kin.
And surely I will never to mortal man give place.
Better it were to perish than to suffer such disgrace."
   With the good swords they began to beat on the helmets
wrought with gold.
Unto the sky went flashing the bright sparks manifold.
Now was there none could part them in the madness of the
fray.
Now it will not be over till one the other slay.

CCLXXXVII. Now Pinabel of Sorence was of excelling
might.
On the Provençal helmet of Thierry did he smite.
The flame leaped from the helmet and set fire unto the sward.
He struck against his foeman with the sharp point of the
sword.
And away from Thierry's forehead all of the helm he clave.
And right before his visage descended the sharp glaive.
All his right cheek was bleeding, and his hauberk slashed in
twain.
To the waist. But God protected him, and Thierry was not
slain.

CCLXXXVIII. And Thierry knew that sorely was he smitten
in the face,
And that his blood was falling on the green grass in the place,
And upon the brown steel helmet he smote Lord Pinabel.
Through the nasal of the helmet the cleaving sword-blade
fell.
And therewith the brain of Pinabel went gushing from his
head.
High, Thierry shook his sword aloft, and smote the champion
dead.
Therewithal the bitter battle in that hour had he won.
Cried all the Franks:
          "A miracle the Lord our God hath done!
It is meet and right that Ganelon should now be hanged on
high;
And likewise all his kinsmen that pled for him shall die."

CCLXXXIX. Now when the champion Thierry had con-
quered in the fray,

With barons four to Charlemagne the King he made his way.
Ogier the Dane and Neimes brought him the King unto,
And likewise William, Lord of Blaye, and Geoffrey of Anjou.
Then did the Emperor Charlemagne Thierry the knight embrace.
With his robe of marten-fur he wiped the blood from off his face.
He doffed the robe. Another they cast his shoulders o'er.
Gently from the brave champion they took the gear of war.
And then they set the hero on a mule of Araby.
And back they rode unto the town in chivalry and glee.
They came to Aix the city, and descended there each one.
And the slaughter of the others thereafter was begun.

CCXC. And then unto his counts and dukes the Emperor
Charlemagne said:
    "What judge ye of my prisoners for Ganelon that pled,
And their bodies for Lord Pinabel as hostages did give?"
And the Franks spake in answer: "Let not any of them live."
    Unto his sheriff Basbrun the Emperor did call:
"Go! unto that accursèd tree see that thou hang them all.
And by this beard whereof the hair is all so hoar and white,
If one escape, on thee the thing with death I will requite."
And Basbrun spake in answer:
                    "What other can I more?"
With an hundred sergeants by main force the men away he
bore.
And there were thirty of them. He hanged them there and
then.
Who so betrayeth, aye he slayeth himself and other men.

CCXCI. Thereafter all the Germans and Bavarians withdrew,
The Bretons and the Normans, and the liegemen of Poitou.
But more than all the others the men of France were fain
That Ganelon should perish in exceeding grievous pain.
They brought four steeds, and unto them they bound his
hands and feet.
Haughty were all the stallions, and very swift and fleet.
Before the steeds to guide them, four servitors did fare
And straight into a meadow wherein there grazed a mare,
Unto horrible destruction Count Ganelon was sent.
The nerves of the man's body unutterably were rent.

And every limb and member from the trunk away was wrenched.
And the flood of his clear life-blood the fair green herbage drenched.
Thus Ganelon came to his death like to a traitor strong.
It is not meet that traitors should boast them in their wrong.

CCXCII. When Charlemagne the Emperor vengeance at last had ta'en,
The Bishops of Bavaria and France and Alamain
He summoned:
                              "In my palace a captive free
doth dwell.
To sermons and fair parables the dame hath hearkened well.
For Christianity she prayeth. On our God she doth believe.
Baptize ye now that Lady that God her soul receive."
    "Then give unto her sponsors," they answered and replied.
Enough there were of ladies of noble race and pride.
There came great press of people to the baths of Aix amain.
By the name of Juliana they baptized the Queen of Spain.
And she herself a Christian most truly did confess.
    When the King had done his justice, appeased was his distress.
In the way of our Christianity Queen Bramimonde had gone.
But now the day passed over and calm the night came on.
And in his vaulted chamber the King lay down to rest,
When to him the angel Gabriel appeared at God's behest:
    "To the hosts of all thine empire, Lord Emperor give command.
Go forth with might and power into the Libyan land.
With succor to King Vivien of Imphè shalt thou ride.
The city that the Paynims have besieged on every side,
Where the Christians call upon thee."
                              Little the King was fain.
"Ah God my life is weary," said the Emperor Charlemagne.
He plucked the white beard hard. The tears down from his eyes they sprang,
And so the great song endeth of the deeds that Therould sang.

Adieu Barons alez voirs que vos amis font Deo Gracias
Le livre des XII pairs est cy finis
Don Louënge a la Saint Trinité.

Notes to Song of Roland

LAISSE LXXVI. The line reading: "And likewise the Lord Olivier who ruleth in his stead" contains an idea not found in the original. Literally the line should be rendered thus: "The Lord Olivier who commands the others."

Laisse LXXIX. That Chaucer was familiar with the story of Ronceveaux goes without saying. His occasional use of the name Ganelon as a synonym for traitor would be sufficient proof, if proof were needed. There is, however, strong presumptive evidence that he was well acquainted with the Song of Roland.

Certain details in the description of Val Neire (the Black Valley) correspond rather remarkably with Chaucer's account of

> "the derke valeye
>   *   *   *   *
> Ther never yet grew corn ne gras,
> Ne tre, ne no thyng that ought was."

This passage is found in the Death of Blanche the Duchess (lines 155–158 Globe edition) and might, considered by itself, be explained as a mere accidental resemblance, but when in lines 1120–1123 of the same poem we come on

> "the false Genellon
> He that purchased the treson
> Of Roland and of Olyvere."

126

the circumstances necessary to such an explanation are indefinitely complicated. I do not think that this faint indication of the direction of Chaucer's literary pilgrimage has been observed heretofore.

Laisse CLXVII. The line reading: "He put great force upon him. And on his feet he got" is supplied from the Venetian manuscript.

Laisse CLXXIII. The line reading: "And in his hand the naked brand, even Durendal, he held" is supplied from the Venetian manuscript.

Laisse CCXXXIV. The line reading: "Of whom was Judas that betrayed his God in sin and shame" is supplied from the Venetian manuscript.

Laisse CCXXXV. "And in the Seventh Column were the Men of Samuel's Race." As far as I know this line offers the only clue from which the date of composition of the poem may be inferred.

Samuel, King of Bulgaria, died in 1014 after a forty-year struggle with Basil the Emperor of the East. The Bulgarians are mentioned in Laisse CCXI. And the hypothesis that this Samuel was the King of Bulgaria is sustained by the fact noted by Leon Gautier that the Heathen Army of Baligant is recruited indiscriminately from the frontiers of Western Christendom. Bulgaria was a great power in the 10th and the 11th centuries. Under Samuel she contested for the mastery of the East with the Byzantine Empire in one of its strongest periods. What more natural than to refer to the Bulgarians as "Samuel's race"?

If the force of this reasoning be admitted and if the Song of Roland as we possess it was written by one man, as the translator for one believes, the poem could not have been written before 976 A.D., the date of Samuel's coronation.

Laisse CCXL. The line reading: "Gigantic was the army that there its way did hold" is supplied from the Venetian manuscript.